S0-BZV-218

THE LIFETIME
FAMILY RECORD BOOK

THE LIFETIME FAMILY RECORD BOOK

A LIVING RECORD FOR YOU

A LEGACY FOR YOUR FAMILY

CROWN PUBLISHERS, INC., NEW YORK

Printed in the United States of America

Published simultaneously in Canada by General Publishing Company Limited

Originally published by the Bruce Lawrence Corporation, North Woodmere, New York 11581

10 9 8 7 6 5 4 3 2

TABLE OF CONTENTS

CONTACT CHECKLIST

Accountant	
Banker	
Doctor	
Employee	
Employer	
Executor	
Family Adviser	
Friends	
Insurance Brokers	
Insurance Company	
Lawyer	
Minister	
Neighbors	
Pension Consultant	
Personnel Department	

Additional Data from Page ____

CONTACT CHECKLIST

Relatives	
Secretary	
Social Security Admin.	
Stockbroker	
Supervisor	
Veterans Admin.	

Additional Data from Page ______

YOUR FAMILY TREE

GENEALOGY—FAMILY MEMBERS

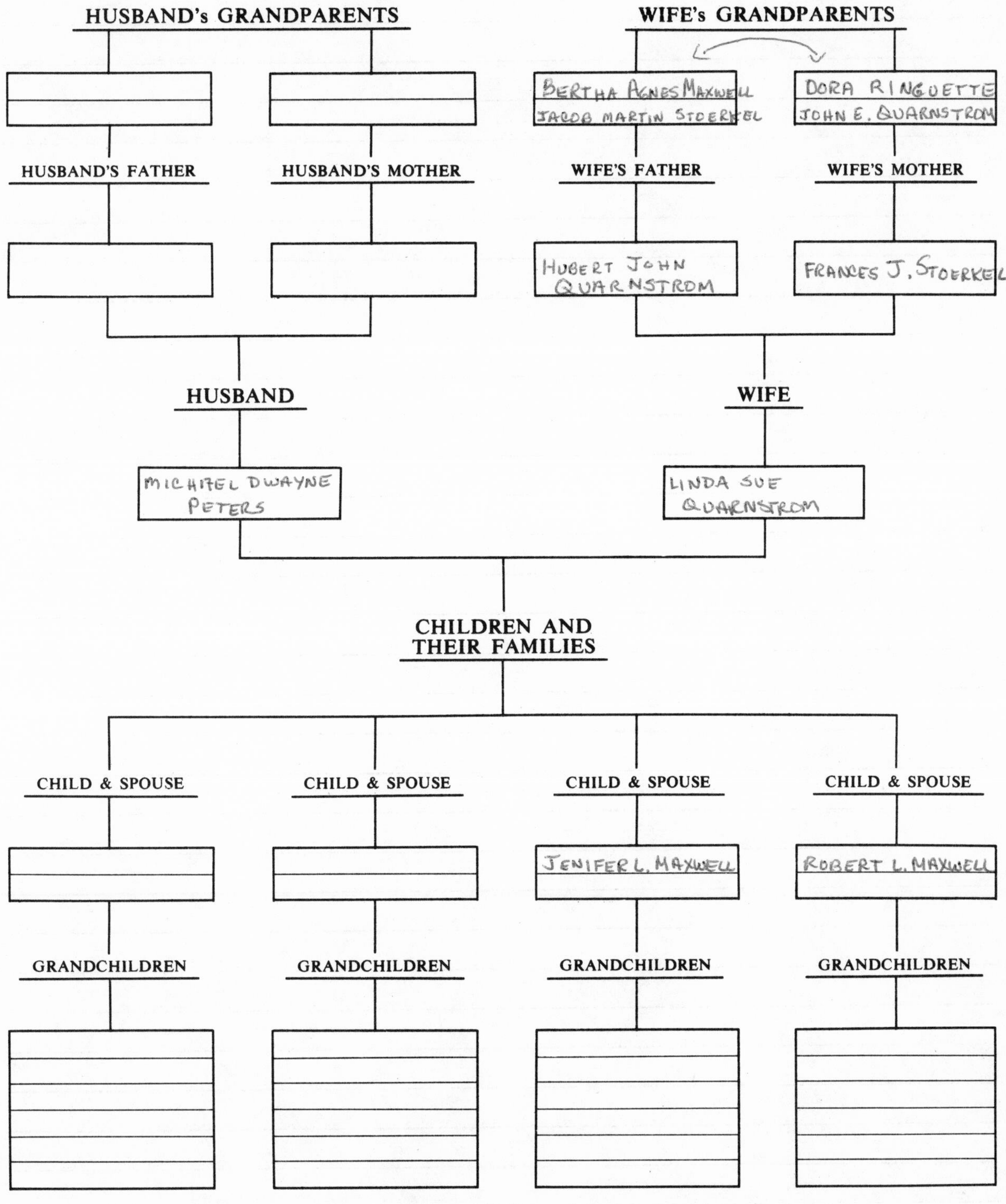
HUSBAND's GRANDPARENTS
WIFE's GRANDPARENTS
BERTHA AGNES MAXWELL
JACOB MARTIN STOERKEL
DORA RINGUETTE
JOHN E. QUARNSTROM
HUSBAND'S FATHER
HUSBAND'S MOTHER
WIFE'S FATHER
WIFE'S MOTHER
HUBERT JOHN QUARNSTROM
FRANCES J. STOERKEL
HUSBAND
WIFE
MICHAEL DWAYNE PETERS
LINDA SUE QUARNSTROM
CHILDREN AND THEIR FAMILIES
CHILD & SPOUSE
CHILD & SPOUSE
CHILD & SPOUSE
CHILD & SPOUSE
JENIFER L. MAXWELL
ROBERT L. MAXWELL
GRANDCHILDREN
GRANDCHILDREN
GRANDCHILDREN
GRANDCHILDREN

Additional Data from Page ______

FAMILY BIRTH INFORMATION

HUSBAND

Date AUGUST 1, 1953

Place of Birth

S.S. # 253-92-9960

WIFE

Date FEBRUARY 10, 1951

Place of Birth CHICAGO, ILLINOIS

S.S. # 259-72-0788

CHILDREN

	AT BIRTH Weight	AT BIRTH Height
Name		
Date		
Place of Birth		
S.S. #		
Name		
Date		
Place of Birth		
S.S. #		
Name		
Date		
Place of Birth		
S.S. #		

	AT BIRTH Weight	AT BIRTH Height
Name JENIFER MAXWELL		
Date 2-15-73		
Place of Birth VICENZA ITALY		
S.S. #		
Name ROBERT MAXWELL		
Date 4-7-78		
Place of Birth EL PASO, TX		
S.S. #		
Name		
Date		
Place of Birth		
S.S. #		

Family member BIRTH CERTIFICATES are KEPT AT:

(Home/ Bank)

Safe Deposit Box #

Bank Branch

Other Place:

Additional Data from Page ____

FAMILY MARRIAGE INFORMATION

We were MARRIED:

Place of Marriage DUNWOODY, GEORGIA

Date 11-25-87

Married by ______

WIFE'S MAIDEN NAME QUARNSTROM

☐ Pre-MARITAL Agreement is Located at ______

☒ Husband ☒ Wife has been DIVORCED or Legally SEPARATED.

HUSBAND

State of Jurisdiction ______

Papers Located at ______

Attorney ______

Tele. ______

Addr. ______

WIFE

State of Jurisdiction GA

Papers Located at CHEROKEE Co.

Attorney STEVE CAMPBELL

Tele. ______

Addr. ______

CHILDREN from PREVIOUS MARRIAGES:
(enter "H" or "W" into box PRECEDING detail line)

☐ Name ______
Birth Date ______

☐ Name ______
Birth Date ______

☐ Name ______
Birth Date ______

☐ Name ______
Birth Date ______

☐ Name ______
Birth Date ______

☐ Name ______
Birth Date ______

RESPONSIBILITY of ESTATE to CHILDREN of PREVIOUS MARRIAGE(S).

Additional Data from Page _____

CHILDREN'S MARRIAGES

Child's Name ________________
Spouse ________________
Bride's Maiden Name ________________
Marriage Date ________________
Place of Marriage ________________
Married by ________________

Child's Name ________________
Spouse ________________
Bride's Maiden Name ________________
Marriage Date ________________
Place of Marriage ________________
Married by ________________

Child's Name ________________
Spouse ________________
Bride's Maiden Name ________________
Marriage Date ________________
Place of Marriage ________________
Married by ________________

Child's Name ________________
Spouse ________________
Bride's Maiden Name ________________
Marriage Date ________________
Place of Marriage ________________
Married by ________________

Child's Name ________________
Spouse ________________
Bride's Maiden Name ________________
Marriage Date ________________
Place of Marriage ________________
Married by ________________

Child's Name ________________
Spouse ________________
Bride's Maiden Name ________________
Marriage Date ________________
Place of Marriage ________________
Married by ________________

Other Information Related to Children's Marriages (In-Laws, etc.)

Additional Data from Page _____

FAMILY MEDICAL HISTORIES

MEDICAL HISTORY OF (family member name) ____________

Regular Physician ____________ Tele. ____________
Surgeon ____________ Tele. ____________
Dentist ____________ Tele. ____________
Ophthalmologist ____________ Tele. ____________

BLOOD TYPE ☐ HEARING ____________ VISION ____________

IMMUNIZATIONS AND TESTS PERFORMED

Type	*Enter Exact Dates, If Known*		
SUCCESSFUL SMALLPOX VACCINATION			
DIPHTHERIA-TETANUS or DIPHTHERIA-TETANUS PERTUSSIS (DPT)			
POLIO: SALK INJECTIONS			
ORAL MONOVALENT			
ORAL TRIVALENT			
MEASLES VACCINE			
RUBELLA (GERMAN MEASLES)			
TUBERCULIN TEST ☐ POSITIVE ☐ NEGATIVE			
BCG VACCINATION			
MUMPS			
INFLUENZA			
OTHER, SPECIFY			

CHECK (✔) if family member had any of the following, where applicable. Enter date next to checked items.

☐ CHICKEN POX
☐ DIPHTHERIA
☐ HEPATITIS
☐ INFLUENZA
☐ MALARIA
☐ MEASLES
☐ MUMPS
☐ PNEUMONIA
☐ POLIO
☐ RUBELLA (German Measles)
☐ SCARLET FEVER
☐ TONSILLITIS
☐ TUBERCULOSIS
☐ TYPHOID
☐ WHOOPING COUGH
☐ ALLERGIES, SPECIFY ____________
☐ OTHER, SPECIFY ____________
☐ OTHER, SPECIFY ____________
☐ OTHER, SPECIFY ____________
☐ OTHER, SPECIFY ____________
☐ OTHER, SPECIFY ____________
☐ HOSP. or SURG. (Diagnosis and Treatment) ____________

PARENTS' MEDICAL HISTORY—Major Illnesses, etc.

____

____

Additional Data from Page _____

FAMILY MEDICAL HISTORY

For __________________________________ Birth Date ________________

HISTORY OF AILMENTS – INOCULATIONS – TREATMENTS, ETC.

Date	*Describe Ailment – Inoculation – Treatment – Drugs, etc.*	*Doctor or Hospital*	*Remarks or Fee*

Additional Data from Page ____

FAMILY MEDICAL HISTORIES

MEDICAL HISTORY OF (family member name) ______________

Regular Physician ______________ Tele. ______________
Surgeon ______________ Tele. ______________
Dentist ______________ Tele. ______________
Ophthalmologist ______________ Tele. ______________

BLOOD TYPE ☐ HEARING ______________ VISION ______________

IMMUNIZATIONS AND TESTS PERFORMED

Type	*Enter Exact Dates, If Known*		
SUCCESSFUL SMALLPOX VACCINATION			
DIPHTHERIA-TETANUS or DIPHTHERIA-TETANUS PERTUSSIS (DPT)			
POLIO: SALK INJECTIONS			
ORAL MONOVALENT			
ORAL TRIVALENT			
MEASLES VACCINE			
RUBELLA (GERMAN MEASLES)			
TUBERCULIN TEST ☐ POSITIVE ☐ NEGATIVE			
BCG VACCINATION			
MUMPS			
INFLUENZA			
OTHER, SPECIFY			

CHECK (✓) if family member had any of the following, where applicable. Enter date next to checked items.

☐ CHICKEN POX
☐ DIPHTHERIA
☐ HEPATITIS
☐ INFLUENZA
☐ MALARIA
☐ MEASLES
☐ MUMPS
☐ PNEUMONIA
☐ POLIO
☐ RUBELLA (German Measles)
☐ SCARLET FEVER
☐ TONSILLITIS
☐ TUBERCULOSIS
☐ TYPHOID
☐ WHOOPING COUGH
☐ ALLERGIES, SPECIFY ______________
☐ OTHER, SPECIFY ______________
☐ OTHER, SPECIFY ______________
☐ OTHER, SPECIFY ______________
☐ OTHER, SPECIFY ______________
☐ OTHER, SPECIFY ______________
☐ HOSP. or SURG. (Diagnosis and Treatment) ______________

PARENTS' MEDICAL HISTORY—Major Illnesses, etc.

____

____

Additional Data from Page _____

FAMILY MEDICAL HISTORY

For ______________________________ Birth Date ______________

HISTORY OF AILMENTS–INOCULATIONS–TREATMENTS, ETC.

Date	*Describe Ailment–Inoculation–Treatment–Drugs, etc.*	*Doctor or Hospital*	*Remarks or Fee*

Additional Data from Page ______

FAMILY MEDICAL HISTORIES

MEDICAL HISTORY OF (family member name) ______________________

Regular Physician ______________________ Tele. ______________

Surgeon ______________________ Tele. ______________

Dentist ______________________ Tele. ______________

Ophthalmologist ______________________ Tele. ______________

BLOOD TYPE ☐ HEARING ______________ VISION ______________

IMMUNIZATIONS AND TESTS PERFORMED

Type	*Enter Exact Dates, If Known*		
SUCCESSFUL SMALLPOX VACCINATION			
DIPHTHERIA-TETANUS or DIPHTHERIA-TETANUS PERTUSSIS (DPT)			
POLIO: SALK INJECTIONS			
ORAL MONOVALENT			
ORAL TRIVALENT			
MEASLES VACCINE			
RUBELLA (GERMAN MEASLES)			
TUBERCULIN TEST ☐ POSITIVE ☐ NEGATIVE			
BCG VACCINATION			
MUMPS			
INFLUENZA			
OTHER, SPECIFY			

CHECK (✔) if family member had any of the following, where applicable. Enter date next to checked items.

☐ CHICKEN POX
☐ DIPHTHERIA
☐ HEPATITIS
☐ INFLUENZA
☐ MALARIA
☐ MEASLES
☐ MUMPS
☐ PNEUMONIA
☐ POLIO
☐ RUBELLA (German Measles)
☐ SCARLET FEVER
☐ TONSILLITIS
☐ TUBERCULOSIS
☐ TYPHOID
☐ WHOOPING COUGH
☐ ALLERGIES, SPECIFY ______________________
☐ OTHER, SPECIFY ______________________
☐ OTHER, SPECIFY ______________________
☐ OTHER, SPECIFY ______________________
☐ OTHER, SPECIFY ______________________
☐ OTHER, SPECIFY ______________________
☐ HOSP. or SURG. (Diagnosis and Treatment) ______________________

PARENTS' MEDICAL HISTORY—Major Illnesses, etc.

____

____

Additional Data from Page _____

FAMILY MEDICAL HISTORY

For ______________________________ Birth Date ______________

HISTORY OF AILMENTS–INOCULATIONS–TREATMENTS, ETC.

Date	*Describe Ailment–Inoculation–Treatment–Drugs, etc.*	*Doctor or Hospital*	*Remarks or Fee*

Additional Data from Page _____

FAMILY MEDICAL HISTORIES

MEDICAL HISTORY OF (family member name) ______________

Regular Physician ______________ Tele. ______________
Surgeon ______________ Tele. ______________
Dentist ______________ Tele. ______________
Ophthalmologist ______________ Tele. ______________

BLOOD TYPE ☐ HEARING ______________ VISION ______________

IMMUNIZATIONS AND TESTS PERFORMED

Type	*Enter Exact Dates, If Known*		
SUCCESSFUL SMALLPOX VACCINATION			
DIPHTHERIA-TETANUS or DIPHTHERIA-TETANUS PERTUSSIS (DPT)			
POLIO: SALK INJECTIONS			
ORAL MONOVALENT			
ORAL TRIVALENT			
MEASLES VACCINE			
RUBELLA (GERMAN MEASLES)			
TUBERCULIN TEST ☐ POSITIVE ☐ NEGATIVE			
BCG VACCINATION			
MUMPS			
INFLUENZA			
OTHER, SPECIFY			

CHECK (✔) if family member had any of the following, where applicable. Enter date next to checked items.

☐ CHICKEN POX ☐ MEASLES ☐ SCARLET FEVER
☐ DIPHTHERIA ☐ MUMPS ☐ TONSILLITIS
☐ HEPATITIS ☐ PNEUMONIA ☐ TUBERCULOSIS
☐ INFLUENZA ☐ POLIO ☐ TYPHOID
☐ MALARIA ☐ RUBELLA (German Measles) ☐ WHOOPING COUGH
☐ ALLERGIES, SPECIFY ______________
☐ OTHER, SPECIFY ______________
☐ OTHER, SPECIFY ______________
☐ OTHER, SPECIFY ______________
☐ OTHER, SPECIFY ______________
☐ OTHER, SPECIFY ______________
☐ HOSP. or SURG. (Diagnosis and Treatment) ______________

PARENTS' MEDICAL HISTORY—Major Illnesses, etc.

____

____

Additional Data from Page ____

FAMILY MEDICAL HISTORY

For ______________________________ Birth Date ______________

HISTORY OF AILMENTS – INOCULATIONS – TREATMENTS, ETC.

Date	*Describe Ailment – Inoculation – Treatment – Drugs, etc.*	*Doctor or Hospital*	*Remarks or Fee*

Additional Data from Page _____

FAMILY MEDICAL HISTORIES

MEDICAL HISTORY OF (family member name) ____________________

Regular Physician ____________________ Tele. ____________
Surgeon ____________________ Tele. ____________
Dentist ____________________ Tele. ____________
Ophthalmologist ____________________ Tele. ____________

BLOOD TYPE [ ] HEARING ____________ VISION ____________

IMMUNIZATIONS AND TESTS PERFORMED

Type	*Enter Exact Dates, If Known*		
SUCCESSFUL SMALLPOX VACCINATION			
DIPHTHERIA-TETANUS or DIPHTHERIA-TETANUS PERTUSSIS (DPT)			
POLIO: SALK INJECTIONS			
ORAL MONOVALENT			
ORAL TRIVALENT			
MEASLES VACCINE			
RUBELLA (GERMAN MEASLES)			
TUBERCULIN TEST ☐ POSITIVE ☐ NEGATIVE			
BCG VACCINATION			
MUMPS			
INFLUENZA			
OTHER, SPECIFY			

CHECK (✓) if family member had any of the following, where applicable. Enter date next to checked items.

☐ CHICKEN POX
☐ DIPHTHERIA
☐ HEPATITIS
☐ INFLUENZA
☐ MALARIA
☐ MEASLES
☐ MUMPS
☐ PNEUMONIA
☐ POLIO
☐ RUBELLA (German Measles)
☐ SCARLET FEVER
☐ TONSILLITIS
☐ TUBERCULOSIS
☐ TYPHOID
☐ WHOOPING COUGH
☐ ALLERGIES, SPECIFY ____________________
☐ OTHER, SPECIFY ____________________
☐ OTHER, SPECIFY ____________________
☐ OTHER, SPECIFY ____________________
☐ OTHER, SPECIFY ____________________
☐ OTHER, SPECIFY ____________________
☐ HOSP. or SURG. (Diagnosis and Treatment) ____________________

PARENTS' MEDICAL HISTORY—Major Illnesses, etc.

____

____

Additional Data from Page ______

FAMILY MEDICAL HISTORY

For ______________________________ Birth Date ______________

HISTORY OF AILMENTS–INOCULATIONS–TREATMENTS, ETC.

Date	*Describe Ailment–Inoculation–Treatment–Drugs, etc.*	*Doctor or Hospital*	*Remarks or Fee*

Additional Data from Page _____

FAMILY MEDICAL HISTORIES

MEDICAL HISTORY OF (family member name) ____________________

Regular Physician ____________________ Tele. ____________

Surgeon ____________________ Tele. ____________

Dentist ____________________ Tele. ____________

Ophthalmologist ____________________ Tele. ____________

BLOOD TYPE [ ] HEARING ____________ VISION ____________

IMMUNIZATIONS AND TESTS PERFORMED

Type	*Enter Exact Dates, If Known*		
SUCCESSFUL SMALLPOX VACCINATION			
DIPHTHERIA-TETANUS or DIPHTHERIA-TETANUS PERTUSSIS (DPT)			
POLIO: SALK INJECTIONS			
ORAL MONOVALENT			
ORAL TRIVALENT			
MEASLES VACCINE			
RUBELLA (GERMAN MEASLES)			
TUBERCULIN TEST ☐ POSITIVE ☐ NEGATIVE			
BCG VACCINATION			
MUMPS			
INFLUENZA			
OTHER, SPECIFY			

CHECK (✔) if family member had any of the following, where applicable. Enter date next to checked items.

☐ CHICKEN POX
☐ DIPHTHERIA
☐ HEPATITIS
☐ INFLUENZA
☐ MALARIA
☐ MEASLES
☐ MUMPS
☐ PNEUMONIA
☐ POLIO
☐ RUBELLA (German Measles)
☐ SCARLET FEVER
☐ TONSILLITIS
☐ TUBERCULOSIS
☐ TYPHOID
☐ WHOOPING COUGH

☐ ALLERGIES, SPECIFY ____________________

☐ OTHER, SPECIFY ____________________

☐ OTHER, SPECIFY ____________________

☐ OTHER, SPECIFY ____________________

☐ OTHER, SPECIFY ____________________

☐ OTHER, SPECIFY ____________________

☐ HOSP. or SURG. (Diagnosis and Treatment) ____________________

PARENTS' MEDICAL HISTORY—Major Illnesses, etc.

____

____

Additional Data from Page _____

FAMILY MEDICAL HISTORY

For ____ Birth Date __________________

HISTORY OF AILMENTS – INOCULATIONS – TREATMENTS, ETC.

Date	*Describe Ailment – Inoculation – Treatment – Drugs, etc.*	*Doctor or Hospital*	*Remarks or Fee*

Additional Data from Page _____

FAMILY ACADEMIC HISTORY

ACADEMIC INSTITUTIONS ATTENDED LOG

This is the schooling history of LINDA QUARNSTROM

NURSERY SCHOOL

School Name ____

Address ____

Tel. Number ____

Dates Attended ____ to ____

GRAMMAR SCHOOL

School Name SEXTON WOODS
Address CHAMBLEE, GA
Tel. Number ____
Dates Attended ____ to ____
Grade Levels 1, 2
(1st, 2nd, 3rd, etc.)

School Name ASHFORD PARK
Address ATLANTA, GA.
Tel. Number ____
Dates Attended ____ to ____
Grade Levels 2, 3, 4, 5, 6, 7
(1st, 2nd, 3rd, etc.)

JUNIOR HIGH SCHOOL

School Name ____
Address ____
Tel. Number ____
Dates Attended ____ to ____
Grade Levels ____

School Name ____
Address ____
Tel. Number ____
Dates Attended ____ to ____
Grade Levels ____

HIGH SCHOOL

School Name CROSS KEYS
Address ATLANTA, GA
Tel. Number ____
Dates Attended 1965 to 1967
Grade Levels 8, 9, 10, 11

~~TECHNICAL SCHOOL~~ HIGH SCHOOL

School Name CHAMBLEE HIGH
Address CHAMBLEE, GA
Tel. Number ____
Dates Attended 1967 to 1969
~~Course of Study~~ GRADE LEVEL 11, 12th

COLLEGE LEVEL

School Name CALHOUN COMM.
Address DECATUR, ALA
Tel. Number ____
Dates Attended 1976 to ____
Major/Minor ____ / ____
Degree ____
G.P.A. (Avg) ____

School Name KENNESAW COLL.
Address KENNESAW, GA
Tel. Number ____
Dates Attended 1984 to 1985
Major/Minor ____ / ____
Degree ____
G.P.A. (Avg) ____

Additional Data from Page _____

FAMILY ACADEMIC HISTORY

RECORD OF ACADEMIC HONORS, ACHIEVEMENTS, EXTRA-CURRICULAR ACTIVITIES

This record belongs to ______________________________

School Name	*Dates Involved*	*Student Year*	*Description of Academic Honors, Achievements, Extra-Curricular Activities, etc.*

OTHER INFORMATION RELATED TO ACADEMICS

Travel (Location and Dates) ______________________________

Books Read ______________________________

Other ______________________________

Additional Data from Page _____

CHILDREN'S ACADEMIC HISTORY
(AND DATA FOR COLLEGE APPLICATIONS)

Child's Name ____________________________

RECORD OF GRADES–SCORES–RANKING

Date of Entry	*Name of School*	*Student Year*	*Period Covered By Grade*	*Subject or Course*	*Grade or Score*	*Remarks Name of Teacher, etc.*

Additional Data from Page ____

FAMILY ACADEMIC HISTORY

ACADEMIC INSTITUTIONS ATTENDED LOG

This is the schooling history of ______________________________

NURSERY SCHOOL

School Name ______________________

Address ______________________

Tel. Number ______________________

Dates Attended __________ to __________

GRAMMAR SCHOOL

School Name ______________

Address ______________

Tel. Number ______________

Dates Attended ______ to ______

Grade Levels ______________
(1st, 2nd, 3rd, etc.)

School Name ______________

Address ______________

Tel. Number ______________

Dates Attended ______ to ______

Grade Levels ______________
(1st, 2nd, 3rd, etc.)

JUNIOR HIGH SCHOOL

School Name ______________

Address ______________

Tel. Number ______________

Dates Attended ______ to ______

Grade Levels ______________

School Name ______________

Address ______________

Tel. Number ______________

Dates Attended ______ to ______

Grade Levels ______________

HIGH SCHOOL

School Name ______________

Address ______________

Tel. Number ______________

Dates Attended ______ to ______

Grade Levels ______________

TECHNICAL SCHOOL

School Name ______________

Address ______________

Tel. Number ______________

Dates Attended ______ to ______

Course of Study ______________

COLLEGE LEVEL

School Name ______________

Address ______________

Tel. Number ______________

Dates Attended ______ to ______

Major/Minor ______/______

Degree ______________

G.P.A. (Avg) ______________

School Name ______________

Address ______________

Tel. Number ______________

Dates Attended ______ to ______

Major/Minor ______/______

Degree ______________

G.P.A. (Avg) ______________

Additional Data from Page _____

FAMILY ACADEMIC HISTORY

RECORD OF ACADEMIC HONORS, ACHIEVEMENTS, EXTRA-CURRICULAR ACTIVITIES

This record belongs to ______________________________

School Name	*Dates Involved*	*Student Year*	*Description of Academic Honors, Achievements, Extra-Curricular Activities, etc.*

OTHER INFORMATION RELATED TO ACADEMICS

Travel (Location and Dates) ______________________________

Books Read ______________________________

Other ______________________________

Additional Data from Page _____

CHILDREN'S ACADEMIC HISTORY
(AND DATA FOR COLLEGE APPLICATIONS)

Child's Name ____________________________

RECORD OF GRADES – SCORES – RANKING

Date of Entry	*Name of School*	*Student Year*	*Period Covered By Grade*	*Subject or Course*	*Grade or Score*	*Remarks Name of Teacher, etc.*

Additional Data from Page _____

FAMILY ACADEMIC HISTORY

ACADEMIC INSTITUTIONS ATTENDED LOG

This is the schooling history of ______________________________

NURSERY SCHOOL

School Name ______________________
Address ______________________
Tel. Number ______________________
Dates Attended __________ to __________

GRAMMAR SCHOOL

School Name ______________
Address ______________
Tel. Number ______________
Dates Attended ______ to ______
Grade Levels ______________
(1st, 2nd, 3rd, etc.)

School Name ______________
Address ______________
Tel. Number ______________
Dates Attended ______ to ______
Grade Levels ______________
(1st, 2nd, 3rd, etc.)

JUNIOR HIGH SCHOOL

School Name ______________
Address ______________
Tel. Number ______________
Dates Attended ______ to ______
Grade Levels ______________

School Name ______________
Address ______________
Tel. Number ______________
Dates Attended ______ to ______
Grade Levels ______________

HIGH SCHOOL

School Name ______________
Address ______________
Tel. Number ______________
Dates Attended ______ to ______
Grade Levels ______________

TECHNICAL SCHOOL

School Name ______________
Address ______________
Tel. Number ______________
Dates Attended ______ to ______
Course of Study ______________

COLLEGE LEVEL

School Name ______________
Address ______________
Tel. Number ______________
Dates Attended ______ to ______
Major/Minor ______/______
Degree ______________
G.P.A. (Avg) ______________

School Name ______________
Address ______________
Tel. Number ______________
Dates Attended ______ to ______
Major/Minor ______/______
Degree ______________
G.P.A. (Avg) ______________

Additional Data from Page _____

FAMILY ACADEMIC HISTORY

RECORD OF ACADEMIC HONORS, ACHIEVEMENTS, EXTRA-CURRICULAR ACTIVITIES

This record belongs to ______________________________

School Name	*Dates Involved*	*Student Year*	*Description of Academic Honors, Achievements, Extra-Curricular Activities, etc.*

OTHER INFORMATION RELATED TO ACADEMICS

Travel (Location and Dates) ______________________________

____

____

Books Read ______________________________

____

____

Other ______________________________

____

Additional Data from Page _____

CHILDREN'S ACADEMIC HISTORY
(AND DATA FOR COLLEGE APPLICATIONS)

Child's Name ______________________________

RECORD OF GRADES–SCORES–RANKING

Date of Entry	*Name of School*	*Student Year*	*Period Covered By Grade*	*Subject or Course*	*Grade or Score*	*Remarks Name of Teacher, etc.*

Additional Data from Page _____

FAMILY ACADEMIC HISTORY

ACADEMIC INSTITUTIONS ATTENDED LOG

This is the schooling history of ______________________________

NURSERY SCHOOL

School Name ______________________________
Address ______________________________
Tel. Number ______________________________
Dates Attended ______________ to ______________

GRAMMAR SCHOOL

School Name ______________________
Address ______________________
Tel. Number ______________________
Dates Attended __________ to __________
Grade Levels ______________________
(1st, 2nd, 3rd, etc.)

School Name ______________________
Address ______________________
Tel. Number ______________________
Dates Attended __________ to __________
Grade Levels ______________________
(1st, 2nd, 3rd, etc.)

JUNIOR HIGH SCHOOL

School Name ______________________
Address ______________________
Tel. Number ______________________
Dates Attended __________ to __________
Grade Levels ______________________

School Name ______________________
Address ______________________
Tel. Number ______________________
Dates Attended __________ to __________
Grade Levels ______________________

HIGH SCHOOL

School Name ______________________
Address ______________________
Tel. Number ______________________
Dates Attended __________ to __________
Grade Levels ______________________

TECHNICAL SCHOOL

School Name ______________________
Address ______________________
Tel. Number ______________________
Dates Attended __________ to __________
Course of Study ______________________

COLLEGE LEVEL

School Name ______________________
Address ______________________
Tel. Number ______________________
Dates Attended __________ to __________
Major/Minor __________/__________
Degree ______________________
G.P.A. (Avg) ______________________

School Name ______________________
Address ______________________
Tel. Number ______________________
Dates Attended __________ to __________
Major/Minor __________/__________
Degree ______________________
G.P.A. (Avg) ______________________

Additional Data from Page _____

FAMILY ACADEMIC HISTORY

RECORD OF ACADEMIC HONORS, ACHIEVEMENTS, EXTRA-CURRICULAR ACTIVITIES

This record belongs to ______________________________

School Name	*Dates Involved*	*Student Year*	*Description of Academic Honors, Achievements, Extra-Curricular Activities, etc.*

OTHER INFORMATION RELATED TO ACADEMICS

Travel (Location and Dates) ______________________________

____

____

Books Read ______________________________

____

____

Other ______________________________

____

Additional Data from Page _____

CHILDREN'S ACADEMIC HISTORY
(AND DATA FOR COLLEGE APPLICATIONS)

Child's Name ______________________________

RECORD OF GRADES–SCORES–RANKING

Date of Entry	*Name of School*	*Student Year*	*Period Covered By Grade*	*Subject or Course*	*Grade or Score*	*Remarks Name of Teacher, etc.*

Additional Data from Page ____

FAMILY ACADEMIC HISTORY

ACADEMIC INSTITUTIONS ATTENDED LOG

This is the schooling history of ______________________

NURSERY SCHOOL

School Name ______________________
Address ______________________
Tel. Number ______________________
Dates Attended ____________ to ____________

GRAMMAR SCHOOL

School Name ______________
Address ______________
Tel. Number ______________
Dates Attended ________ to ________
Grade Levels ______________
(1st, 2nd, 3rd, etc.)

School Name ______________
Address ______________
Tel. Number ______________
Dates Attended ________ to ________
Grade Levels ______________
(1st, 2nd, 3rd, etc.)

JUNIOR HIGH SCHOOL

School Name ______________
Address ______________
Tel. Number ______________
Dates Attended ________ to ________
Grade Levels ______________

School Name ______________
Address ______________
Tel. Number ______________
Dates Attended ________ to ________
Grade Levels ______________

HIGH SCHOOL

School Name ______________
Address ______________
Tel. Number ______________
Dates Attended ________ to ________
Grade Levels ______________

TECHNICAL SCHOOL

School Name ______________
Address ______________
Tel. Number ______________
Dates Attended ________ to ________
Course of Study ______________

COLLEGE LEVEL

School Name ______________
Address ______________
Tel. Number ______________
Dates Attended ________ to ________
Major/Minor ______/______
Degree ______________
G.P.A. (Avg) ______________

School Name ______________
Address ______________
Tel. Number ______________
Dates Attended ________ to ________
Major/Minor ______/______
Degree ______________
G.P.A. (Avg) ______________

Additional Data from Page _____

FAMILY ACADEMIC HISTORY

RECORD OF ACADEMIC HONORS, ACHIEVEMENTS, EXTRA-CURRICULAR ACTIVITIES

This record belongs to ______________________________

School Name	*Dates Involved*	*Student Year*	*Description of Academic Honors, Achievements, Extra-Curricular Activities, etc.*

OTHER INFORMATION RELATED TO ACADEMICS

Travel (Location and Dates) ______________________________

Books Read ______________________________

Other ______________________________

Additional Data from Page _____

CHILDREN'S ACADEMIC HISTORY
(AND DATA FOR COLLEGE APPLICATIONS)

Child's Name ______________________

RECORD OF GRADES–SCORES–RANKING

Date of Entry	*Name of School*	*Student Year*	*Period Covered By Grade*	*Subject or Course*	*Grade or Score*	*Remarks Name of Teacher, etc.*

Additional Data from Page _____

MILITARY SERVICE HISTORY

NAME: ______________________ SERIAL #: ________________

	Dates	*Unit/Theater/Base*
Enlistment/Induction		
Basic Training/Boot Camp		
Special Training		

Service Record

Date	*Rank*	*Unit/Theater*

Citations/Awards

Date	*Award*	

Service Related Disabilities

Type	*Monthly Amount*

Additional Data from Page _____

MILITARY SERVICE HISTORY

NAME: ______________________________

Highlights/Memorabilia

Date	

Separation/Reserve Information

	Date	*Military Post/Unit*
Separation		
Reserve		

Discharge Papers Located: ______________________________

Additional Data from Page _____

MILITARY SERVICE HISTORY

COMRADES IN ARMS/ACQUAINTANCES

Name	*Rank*	*Address/Phone*

Additional Data from Page _____

EMPLOYMENT RECORD

PERSONAL EMPLOYMENT—HUSBAND

EMPLOYER ______________________
Address ______________________
____
Telephone ______________________

☐ Corporation
☐ Partnership
☐ Individual Proprietorship
SALARY ____________

Immediate Supervisor is:
Name ______________________
Title ______________________
Tele. ______________________

Employment Commenced ___/___/___
Employment Contract ☐ YES
☐ NO

Employer has the following benefit plans in which I participate (CHECK):

☐ Blue Cross
☐ Blue Shield
☐ Major Medical (Company) ________
☐ Pension Plan
☐ Accident Insurance
☐ Disability Plan
☐ Other ______________

☐ Prescription
☐ Dental
☐ Credit Union
☐ Profit Sharing
☐ Stock Purchase
☐ Life Insurance $ ____________
☐ Other ______________

Benefit Plan Administrator:
Name ______________________
Title ______________________
Tele. ______________________

Benefit Plan Booklets are at:
____
____
☐ Safe Dep. Box # ______ ☐ Safe

Union Member ☐ NO ☐ YES, Local Number ____________.
Union Benefits ☐ NO ☐ YES, they are: ____________
____
____
Union Name ______________________
Tele. No. ______________________

Personal Items in Office at Employer:

______________________ ______________________
______________________ ______________________
______________________ ______________________
______________________ ______________________

☐ Resigned ☐ Terminated ☐ Retired on ___/___/___

Additional Data from Page _____

EMPLOYMENT RECORD

PERSONAL EMPLOYMENT—HUSBAND

EMPLOYER ______________________

Address ______________________

____

Telephone ______________________

☐ Corporation
☐ Partnership
☐ Individual Proprietorship

SALARY ____________

Immediate Supervisor is:

Name ______________________

Title ______________________

Tele. ______________________

Employment Commenced ___/___/___

Employment Contract ☐ YES
☐ NO

Employer has the following benefit plans in which I participate (CHECK):

☐ Blue Cross
☐ Blue Shield
☐ Major Medical (Company) ________
☐ Pension Plan
☐ Accident Insurance
☐ Disability Plan
☐ Other ______________

☐ Prescription
☐ Dental
☐ Credit Union
☐ Profit Sharing
☐ Stock Purchase
☐ Life Insurance $ ____________
☐ Other ______________

Benefit Plan Administrator:

Name ______________________

Title ______________________

Tele. ______________________

Benefit Plan Booklets are at:

____

____

☐ Safe Dep. Box # ______ ☐ Safe

Union Member ☐ NO ☐ YES, Local Number ____________.

Union Benefits ☐ NO ☐ YES, they are: { ______________________ / ______________________ / ______________________

Union Name ______________________

Tele. No. ______________________

Personal Items in Office at Employer:

______________________ ______________________

______________________ ______________________

______________________ ______________________

______________________ ______________________

☐ Resigned ☐ Terminated ☐ Retired on ___/___/___

Additional Data from Page _____

EMPLOYMENT RECORD

PERSONAL EMPLOYMENT–HUSBAND

EMPLOYER ______________________

Address ______________________

____

Telephone ______________________

☐ Corporation

☐ Partnership

☐ Individual Proprietorship

SALARY ____________

Immediate Supervisor is:

Name ______________________

Title ______________________

Tele. ______________________

Employment Commenced ___/___/___

Employment Contract ☐ YES

☐ NO

Employer has the following benefit plans in which I participate (CHECK):

☐ Blue Cross

☐ Blue Shield

☐ Major Medical (Company) ________

☐ Pension Plan

☐ Accident Insurance

☐ Disability Plan

☐ Other ______________________

☐ Prescription

☐ Dental

☐ Credit Union

☐ Profit Sharing

☐ Stock Purchase

☐ Life Insurance $ ____________

☐ Other ______________________

Benefit Plan Administrator:

Name ______________________

Title ______________________

Tele. ______________________

Benefit Plan Booklets are at:

____

____

☐ Safe Dep. Box # ______ ☐ Safe

Union Member ☐ NO ☐ YES, Local Number ____________.

Union Benefits ☐ NO ☐ YES, they are: ______________________

____

____

Union Name ______________________

Tele. No. ______________________

Personal Items in Office at Employer:

______________________ ______________________

______________________ ______________________

______________________ ______________________

______________________ ______________________

☐ Resigned ☐ Terminated ☐ Retired on ___/___/___

Additional Data from Page _____

EMPLOYMENT RECORD

PERSONAL EMPLOYMENT–HUSBAND

EMPLOYER ______________________
Address ______________________
____
Telephone ______________________

☐ Corporation
☐ Partnership
☐ Individual Proprietorship
SALARY ______________

Immediate Supervisor is:
Name ______________________
Title ______________________
Tele. ______________________

Employment Commenced ___/___/___
Employment Contract ☐ YES
☐ NO

Employer has the following benefit plans in which I participate (CHECK):

☐ Blue Cross
☐ Blue Shield
☐ Major Medical (Company) ________
☐ Pension Plan
☐ Accident Insurance
☐ Disability Plan
☐ Other ______________________

☐ Prescription
☐ Dental
☐ Credit Union
☐ Profit Sharing
☐ Stock Purchase
☐ Life Insurance $ ______________
☐ Other ______________________

Benefit Plan Administrator:
Name ______________________
Title ______________________
Tele. ______________________

Benefit Plan Booklets are at:
____
____
☐ Safe Dep. Box # ______ ☐ Safe

Union Member ☐ NO ☐ YES, Local Number ______________.
Union Benefits ☐ NO ☐ YES, they are: ______________________
____
____
Union Name ______________________
Tele. No. ______________________

Personal Items in Office at Employer:

______________________ ______________________
______________________ ______________________
______________________ ______________________
______________________ ______________________

☐ Resigned ☐ Terminated ☐ Retired on ___/___/___

Additional Data from Page _____

EMPLOYMENT RECORD

PERSONAL EMPLOYMENT—WIFE

EMPLOYER ______________________
Address ______________________
____
Telephone ______________________

☐ Corporation
☐ Partnership
☐ Individual Proprietorship
SALARY ______________

Immediate Supervisor is:
Name ______________________
Title ______________________
Tele. ______________________

Employment Commenced ___/___/___
Employment Contract ☐ YES
☐ NO

Employer has the following benefit plans in which I participate (CHECK):

☐ Blue Cross
☐ Blue Shield
☐ Major Medical (Company) __________
☐ Pension Plan
☐ Accident Insurance
☐ Disability Plan
☐ Other ______________________

☐ Prescription
☐ Dental
☐ Credit Union
☐ Profit Sharing
☐ Stock Purchase
☐ Life Insurance $ ______________
☐ Other ______________________

Benefit Plan Administrator:
Name ______________________
Title ______________________
Tele. ______________________

Benefit Plan Booklets are at:
____
____
☐ Safe Dep. Box # ______ ☐ Safe

Union Member ☐ NO ☐ YES, Local Number ______________.
Union Benefits ☐ NO ☐ YES, they are:
____
____
____
Union Name ______________________
Tele. No. ______________________

Personal Items in Office at Employer:

______________________ ______________________
______________________ ______________________
______________________ ______________________
______________________ ______________________

☐ Resigned ☐ Terminated ☐ Retired on ___/___/___

Additional Data from Page _____

EMPLOYMENT RECORD

PERSONAL EMPLOYMENT—WIFE

EMPLOYER ______________________ ☐ Corporation
Address ______________________ ☐ Partnership
______________________ ☐ Individual Proprietorship
Telephone ______________________ SALARY __________

Immediate Supervisor is:
Name ______________________
Title ______________________
Tele. ______________________

Employment Commenced ___/___/___
Employment Contract ☐ YES
☐ NO

Employer has the following benefit plans in which I participate (CHECK):

☐ Blue Cross
☐ Blue Shield
☐ Major Medical (Company) __________
☐ Pension Plan
☐ Accident Insurance
☐ Disability Plan
☐ Other ______________________
☐ Prescription
☐ Dental
☐ Credit Union
☐ Profit Sharing
☐ Stock Purchase
☐ Life Insurance $ __________
☐ Other ______________________

Benefit Plan Administrator:
Name ______________________
Title ______________________
Tele. ______________________

Benefit Plan Booklets are at:
____
____
☐ Safe Dep. Box # ______ ☐ Safe

Union Member ☐ NO ☐ YES, Local Number __________.
Union Benefits ☐ NO ☐ YES, they are: ______________________
____
____
Union Name ______________________
Tele. No. ______________________

Personal Items in Office at Employer:

______________________ ______________________
______________________ ______________________
______________________ ______________________
______________________ ______________________

☐ Resigned ☐ Terminated ☐ Retired on ___/___/___

Additional Data from Page _____

EMPLOYMENT RECORD

PERSONAL EMPLOYMENT—WIFE

EMPLOYER ____________________ ☐ Corporation
Address ____________________ ☐ Partnership
____________________ ☐ Individual Proprietorship
Telephone ____________________ SALARY ____________

Immediate Supervisor is:
Name ____________________
Title ____________________
Tele. ____________________

Employment Commenced ___/___/___
Employment Contract ☐ YES
☐ NO

Employer has the following benefit plans in which I participate (CHECK):

☐ Blue Cross
☐ Blue Shield
☐ Major Medical (Company) ________
☐ Pension Plan
☐ Accident Insurance
☐ Disability Plan
☐ Other ____________________
☐ Prescription
☐ Dental
☐ Credit Union
☐ Profit Sharing
☐ Stock Purchase
☐ Life Insurance $ ____________
☐ Other ____________________

Benefit Plan Administrator:
Name ____________________
Title ____________________
Tele. ____________________

Benefit Plan Booklets are at:
____
____
☐ Safe Dep. Box # ______ ☐ Safe

Union Member ☐ NO ☐ YES, Local Number ____________.
Union Benefits ☐ NO ☐ YES, they are: { ____________________ / ____________________ / ____________________
Union Name ____________________
Tele. No. ____________________

Personal Items in Office at Employer:

____________________ ____________________
____________________ ____________________
____________________ ____________________
____________________ ____________________

☐ Resigned ☐ Terminated ☐ Retired on ___/___/___

Additional Data from Page _____

EMPLOYMENT RECORD

PERSONAL EMPLOYMENT—CHILDREN

Child's Name ______________________
Employer ______________________
Address ______________________
____
Tel. Number ______________________
Date Employed ______________________

IMMEDIATE SUPERVISOR IS:

Name ______________________
Title ______________________
Tel. Number ______________________

Child's Name ______________________
Employer ______________________
Address ______________________
____
Tel. Number ______________________
Date Employed ______________________

IMMEDIATE SUPERVISOR IS:

Name ______________________
Title ______________________
Tel. Number ______________________

Child's Name ______________________
Employer ______________________
Address ______________________
____
Tel. Number ______________________
Date Employed ______________________

IMMEDIATE SUPERVISOR IS:

Name ______________________
Title ______________________
Tel. Number ______________________

Child's Name ______________________
Employer ______________________
Address ______________________
____
Tel. Number ______________________
Date Employed ______________________

IMMEDIATE SUPERVISOR IS:

Name ______________________
Title ______________________
Tel. Number ______________________

Child's Name ______________________
Employer ______________________
Address ______________________
____
Tel. Number ______________________
Date Employed ______________________

IMMEDIATE SUPERVISOR IS:

Name ______________________
Title ______________________
Tel. Number ______________________

Child's Name ______________________
Employer ______________________
Address ______________________
____
Tel. Number ______________________
Date Employed ______________________

IMMEDIATE SUPERVISOR IS:

Name ______________________
Title ______________________
Tel. Number ______________________

Additional Data from Page _____

BUSINESS AFFILIATIONS

BUSINESS AFFILIATIONS—BUSINESS OWNERSHIP (HUSBAND)

Business Ownership in the Following:

Name and Address of Business	*Nature and Type of Business*	*% Ownership*

The Following Business Documents are Located at:

- ☐ Certificate of Doing Business ____________
- ☐ Partnership Agreement ____________
- ☐ Stockholders Agreement ____________
- ☐ Survivors Agreement ____________
- ☐ Stock Certificates ____________
- ☐ Options ____________
- ☐ Registration Statements ____________
- ☐ Other ____________ ____________

Business Partners or Fellow Stockholders are:

Name	*% Interest*	*Name*	*% Interest*

Business Attorney is:
Name ____________
Addr. ____________
____
Tele. ____________

Business Accountant is:
Name ____________
Addr. ____________
____
Tele. ____________

In the event of death, contact the following person for my desired disposition of business interests:

Name ____________
Addr. ____________
____
Tele. ____________

Person whose advice I consider best about my business is:
Name ____________
Tele. ____________
Addr. ____________
____

Additional Data from Page _____

BUSINESS AFFILIATIONS

BUSINESS AFFILIATIONS–BUSINESS OWNERSHIP (WIFE)

Business Ownership in the Following:

Name and Address of Business	*Nature and Type of Business*	*% Ownership*

The Following Business Documents are Located at:

- ☐ Certificate of Doing Business ______
- ☐ Partnership Agreement ______
- ☐ Stockholders Agreement ______
- ☐ Survivors Agreement ______
- ☐ Stock Certificates ______
- ☐ Options ______
- ☐ Registration Statements ______
- ☐ Other ______ ______

Business Partners or Fellow Stockholders are:

Name	*% Interest*	*Name*	*% Interest*

Business Attorney is:
Name ______
Addr. ______
______
Tele. ______

Business Accountant is:
Name ______
Addr. ______
______
Tele. ______

In the event of death, contact the following person for my desired disposition of business interests:

Name ______
Addr. ______
______
Tele. ______

Person whose advice I consider best about my business is:
Name ______
Tele. ______
Addr. ______
______

Additional Data from Page _____

BANKING INFORMATION

CHECKING AND SAVINGS ACCOUNTS

☐ Savings ☐ Checking
Account # ____________
Account Name ____________
Bank Name ____________
Bank Addr. ____________
____
Bank Tele. ____________

☐ Savings ☐ Checking
Account # ____________
Account Name ____________
Bank Name ____________
Bank Addr. ____________
____
Bank Tele. ____________

☐ Savings ☐ Checking
Account # ____________
Account Name ____________
Bank Name ____________
Bank Addr. ____________
____
Bank Tele. ____________

☐ Savings ☐ Checking
Account # ____________
Account Name ____________
Bank Name ____________
Bank Addr. ____________
____
Bank Tele. ____________

☐ Savings ☐ Checking
Account # ____________
Account Name ____________
Bank Name ____________
Bank Addr. ____________
____
Bank Tele. ____________

☐ Savings ☐ Checking
Account # ____________
Account Name ____________
Bank Name ____________
Bank Addr. ____________
____
Bank Tele. ____________

Savings Account Bank Books are Located at ____________
____

A POWER OF ATTORNEY issued on ___/___/___ until ___/___/___ authorizes ____________ to sign Checks, open Safe Deposit Boxes, Withdraw Monies, etc.

The following Savings Accounts are being held as Security:

Account Number	*Bank*	*Held By*	*Reason*	*Amt.*

Additional Data from Page _____

BANKING INFORMATION

CHECKING AND SAVINGS ACCOUNTS

☐ Savings ☐ Checking
Account # ____________
Account Name ____________
Bank Name ____________
Bank Addr. ____________
____
Bank Tele. ____________

☐ Savings ☐ Checking
Account # ____________
Account Name ____________
Bank Name ____________
Bank Addr. ____________
____
Bank Tele. ____________

☐ Savings ☐ Checking
Account # ____________
Account Name ____________
Bank Name ____________
Bank Addr. ____________
____
Bank Tele. ____________

☐ Savings ☐ Checking
Account # ____________
Account Name ____________
Bank Name ____________
Bank Addr. ____________
____
Bank Tele. ____________

☐ Savings ☐ Checking
Account # ____________
Account Name ____________
Bank Name ____________
Bank Addr. ____________
____
Bank Tele. ____________

☐ Savings ☐ Checking
Account # ____________
Account Name ____________
Bank Name ____________
Bank Addr. ____________
____
Bank Tele. ____________

Savings Account Bank Books are Located at ____________
____

A POWER OF ATTORNEY issued on ___/___/___ until ___/___/___ authorizes ____________ to sign Checks, open Safe Deposit Boxes, Withdraw Monies, etc.

The following Savings Accounts are being held as Security:

Account Number	*Bank*	*Held By*	*Reason*	*Amt.*

Additional Data from Page ____

BANKING INFORMATION

CHECKING AND SAVINGS ACCOUNTS

☐ Savings ☐ Checking
Account # ____________
Account Name ____________
Bank Name ____________
Bank Addr. ____________
____
Bank Tele. ____________

☐ Savings ☐ Checking
Account # ____________
Account Name ____________
Bank Name ____________
Bank Addr. ____________
____
Bank Tele. ____________

☐ Savings ☐ Checking
Account # ____________
Account Name ____________
Bank Name ____________
Bank Addr. ____________
____
Bank Tele. ____________

☐ Savings ☐ Checking
Account # ____________
Account Name ____________
Bank Name ____________
Bank Addr. ____________
____
Bank Tele. ____________

☐ Savings ☐ Checking
Account # ____________
Account Name ____________
Bank Name ____________
Bank Addr. ____________
____
Bank Tele. ____________

☐ Savings ☐ Checking
Account # ____________
Account Name ____________
Bank Name ____________
Bank Addr. ____________
____
Bank Tele. ____________

Savings Account Bank Books are Located at ____________
____

A POWER OF ATTORNEY issued on ___/___/___ until ___/___/___ authorizes ____________ to sign Checks, open Safe Deposit Boxes, Withdraw Monies, etc.

The following Savings Accounts are being held as Security:

Account Number	*Bank*	*Held By*	*Reason*	*Amt.*

Additional Data from Page ____

BANKING INFORMATION

PERSONAL/BANK LOANS

Type of Loan ______________________
Amount of Loan ______________________
When Due ______________________
Payable to ______________________
Interest Rate ______________________
Security, if any ______________________
Security held by ______________________
Fully Repaid ☐ Yes ☐ No

Type of Loan ______________________
Amount of Loan ______________________
When Due ______________________
Payable to ______________________
Interest Rate ______________________
Security, if any ______________________
Security held by ______________________
Fully Repaid ☐ Yes ☐ No

Type of Loan ______________________
Amount of Loan ______________________
When Due ______________________
Payable to ______________________
Interest Rate ______________________
Security, if any ______________________
Security held by ______________________
Fully Repaid ☐ Yes ☐ No

Type of Loan ______________________
Amount of Loan ______________________
When Due ______________________
Payable to ______________________
Interest Rate ______________________
Security, if any ______________________
Security held by ______________________
Fully Repaid ☐ Yes ☐ No

Type of Loan ______________________
Amount of Loan ______________________
When Due ______________________
Payable to ______________________
Interest Rate ______________________
Security, if any ______________________
Security held by ______________________
Fully Repaid ☐ Yes ☐ No

Type of Loan ______________________
Amount of Loan ______________________
When Due ______________________
Payable to ______________________
Interest Rate ______________________
Security, if any ______________________
Security held by ______________________
Fully Repaid ☐ Yes ☐ No

Type of Loan ______________________
Amount of Loan ______________________
When Due ______________________
Payable to ______________________
Interest Rate ______________________
Security, if any ______________________
Security held by ______________________
Fully Repaid ☐ Yes ☐ No

Type of Loan ______________________
Amount of Loan ______________________
When Due ______________________
Payable to ______________________
Interest Rate ______________________
Security, if any ______________________
Security held by ______________________
Fully Repaid ☐ Yes ☐ No

Additional Data from Page _____

BANKING INFORMATION

PERSONAL/BANK LOANS

Type of Loan ______________________
Amount of Loan ______________________
When Due ______________________
Payable to ______________________
Interest Rate ______________________
Security, if any ______________________
Security held by ______________________
Fully Repaid ☐ Yes ☐ No

Type of Loan ______________________
Amount of Loan ______________________
When Due ______________________
Payable to ______________________
Interest Rate ______________________
Security, if any ______________________
Security held by ______________________
Fully Repaid ☐ Yes ☐ No

Type of Loan ______________________
Amount of Loan ______________________
When Due ______________________
Payable to ______________________
Interest Rate ______________________
Security, if any ______________________
Security held by ______________________
Fully Repaid ☐ Yes ☐ No

Type of Loan ______________________
Amount of Loan ______________________
When Due ______________________
Payable to ______________________
Interest Rate ______________________
Security, if any ______________________
Security held by ______________________
Fully Repaid ☐ Yes ☐ No

Type of Loan ______________________
Amount of Loan ______________________
When Due ______________________
Payable to ______________________
Interest Rate ______________________
Security, if any ______________________
Security held by ______________________
Fully Repaid ☐ Yes ☐ No

Type of Loan ______________________
Amount of Loan ______________________
When Due ______________________
Payable to ______________________
Interest Rate ______________________
Security, if any ______________________
Security held by ______________________
Fully Repaid ☐ Yes ☐ No

Type of Loan ______________________
Amount of Loan ______________________
When Due ______________________
Payable to ______________________
Interest Rate ______________________
Security, if any ______________________
Security held by ______________________
Fully Repaid ☐ Yes ☐ No

Type of Loan ______________________
Amount of Loan ______________________
When Due ______________________
Payable to ______________________
Interest Rate ______________________
Security, if any ______________________
Security held by ______________________
Fully Repaid ☐ Yes ☐ No

Additional Data from Page _____

BANKING INFORMATION

PERSONAL/BANK LOANS

Type of Loan ______________________
Amount of Loan ______________________
When Due ______________________
Payable to ______________________
Interest Rate ______________________
Security, if any ______________________
Security held by ______________________
Fully Repaid ☐ Yes ☐ No

Type of Loan ______________________
Amount of Loan ______________________
When Due ______________________
Payable to ______________________
Interest Rate ______________________
Security, if any ______________________
Security held by ______________________
Fully Repaid ☐ Yes ☐ No

Type of Loan ______________________
Amount of Loan ______________________
When Due ______________________
Payable to ______________________
Interest Rate ______________________
Security, if any ______________________
Security held by ______________________
Fully Repaid ☐ Yes ☐ No

Type of Loan ______________________
Amount of Loan ______________________
When Due ______________________
Payable to ______________________
Interest Rate ______________________
Security, if any ______________________
Security held by ______________________
Fully Repaid ☐ Yes ☐ No

Type of Loan ______________________
Amount of Loan ______________________
When Due ______________________
Payable to ______________________
Interest Rate ______________________
Security, if any ______________________
Security held by ______________________
Fully Repaid ☐ Yes ☐ No

Type of Loan ______________________
Amount of Loan ______________________
When Due ______________________
Payable to ______________________
Interest Rate ______________________
Security, if any ______________________
Security held by ______________________
Fully Repaid ☐ Yes ☐ No

Type of Loan ______________________
Amount of Loan ______________________
When Due ______________________
Payable to ______________________
Interest Rate ______________________
Security, if any ______________________
Security held by ______________________
Fully Repaid ☐ Yes ☐ No

Type of Loan ______________________
Amount of Loan ______________________
When Due ______________________
Payable to ______________________
Interest Rate ______________________
Security, if any ______________________
Security held by ______________________
Fully Repaid ☐ Yes ☐ No

Additional Data from Page _____

INSURANCE LOG

FAMILY LIFE INSURANCE POLICIES

Family Life Insurance Advisor is ____________________

Addr. ____________________

Tele. ____________ ____________________

(NOTE: Type = Straight/Whole Life, Term, Annuity, Endowment, etc.)

Life of ____________________ Company ________
Face Value ________ Policy Owner ________ Policy Number ________
Type ________ Expires On ________ Premiums ________

Life of ____________________ Company ________
Face Value ________ Policy Owner ________ Policy Number ________
Type ________ Expires On ________ Premiums ________

Life of ____________________ Company ________
Face Value ________ Policy Owner ________ Policy Number ________
Type ________ Expires On ________ Premiums ________

Life of ____________________ Company ________
Face Value ________ Policy Owner ________ Policy Number ________
Type ________ Expires On ________ Premiums ________

Life of ____________________ Company ________
Face Value ________ Policy Owner ________ Policy Number ________
Type ________ Expires On ________ Premiums ________

Life of ____________________ Company ________
Face Value ________ Policy Owner ________ Policy Number ________
Type ________ Expires On ________ Premiums ________

Life of ____________________ Company ________
Face Value ________ Policy Owner ________ Policy Number ________
Type ________ Expires On ________ Premiums ________

Additional Data from Page _____

INSURANCE LOG

FAMILY LIFE INSURANCE POLICIES

Family Life Insurance Advisor is ______________________

Addr. ______________________

Tele. ______________ ______________________

(NOTE: Type = Straight/Whole Life, Term, Annuity, Endowment, etc.)

Life of ______________________ Company __________
Face Value __________ Policy Owner __________ Policy Number __________
Type __________ Expires On __________ Premiums __________

Life of ______________________ Company __________
Face Value __________ Policy Owner __________ Policy Number __________
Type __________ Expires On __________ Premiums __________

Life of ______________________ Company __________
Face Value __________ Policy Owner __________ Policy Number __________
Type __________ Expires On __________ Premiums __________

Life of ______________________ Company __________
Face Value __________ Policy Owner __________ Policy Number __________
Type __________ Expires On __________ Premiums __________

Life of ______________________ Company __________
Face Value __________ Policy Owner __________ Policy Number __________
Type __________ Expires On __________ Premiums __________

Life of ______________________ Company __________
Face Value __________ Policy Owner __________ Policy Number __________
Type __________ Expires On __________ Premiums __________

Life of ______________________ Company __________
Face Value __________ Policy Owner __________ Policy Number __________
Type __________ Expires On __________ Premiums __________

Additional Data from Page _____

INSURANCE LOG

FAMILY HOMEOWNERS INSURANCE POLICIES

Location Insured is ______________________ Policy Number __________
Company __________ Expires On __________ Premiums __________
Jewelry/Fur Floater* Broker is ____________________
☐ YES ☐ NO Tele. Number ____________________

Location Insured is ______________________ Policy Number __________
Company __________ Expires On __________ Premiums __________
Jewelry/Fur Floater* Broker is ____________________
☐ YES ☐ NO Tele. Number ____________________

Location Insured is ______________________ Policy Number __________
Company __________ Expires On __________ Premiums __________
Jewelry/Fur Floater* Broker is ____________________
☐ YES ☐ NO Tele. Number ____________________

Location Insured is ______________________ Policy Number __________
Company __________ Expires On __________ Premiums __________
Jewelry/Fur Floater* Broker is ____________________
☐ YES ☐ NO Tele. Number ____________________

Location Insured is ______________________ Policy Number __________
Company __________ Expires On __________ Premiums __________
Jewelry/Fur Floater* Broker is ____________________
☐ YES ☐ NO Tele. Number ____________________

* Jewelry/Fur Floater, list items covered by such floaters in above policies

Description	*Value*	*Description*	*Value*

Additional Data from Page ____

INSURANCE LOG

FAMILY HOMEOWNERS INSURANCE POLICIES

Location Insured is ______________________ Policy Number __________
Company __________ Expires On __________ Premiums __________
Jewelry/Fur Floater* Broker is ____________________
☐ YES ☐ NO Tele. Number ____________________

Location Insured is ______________________ Policy Number __________
Company __________ Expires On __________ Premiums __________
Jewelry/Fur Floater* Broker is ____________________
☐ YES ☐ NO Tele. Number ____________________

Location Insured is ______________________ Policy Number __________
Company __________ Expires On __________ Premiums __________
Jewelry/Fur Floater* Broker is ____________________
☐ YES ☐ NO Tele. Number ____________________

Location Insured is ______________________ Policy Number __________
Company __________ Expires On __________ Premiums __________
Jewelry/Fur Floater* Broker is ____________________
☐ YES ☐ NO Tele. Number ____________________

Location Insured is ______________________ Policy Number __________
Company __________ Expires On __________ Premiums __________
Jewelry/Fur Floater* Broker is ____________________
☐ YES ☐ NO Tele. Number ____________________

* Jewelry/Fur Floater, list items covered by such floaters in above policies

Description	*Value*	*Description*	*Value*

Additional Data from Page _____

INSURANCE LOG

FAMILY AUTOMOBILE INSURANCE POLICIES

Policy Covers	*Expires*	*Policy No.*	*Ins. Company*	*Ins. Broker*

HEALTH INSURANCE COVERAGE

Policy Description	*Benefits Provided*	*Company*

OTHER FAMILY INSURANCE POLICIES

Policy Description	*Expires*	*Policy No.*	*Ins. Company*	*Ins. Broker*

INSURANCE POLICIES ARE LOCATED AT

____

____

____

Additional Data from Page ____

TRUST FUNDS

The following is a List of FAMILY Trust Funds:

Benefit of ____________________

Established On ____________________

Trust Agreement Located ____________________

Trustees are ____________________

____

The Lawyer or Bank who drew the Trust Agreement is:

Name ____________________

Addr. ____________________

____

Tele. ____________________

Benefit of ____________________

Established On ____________________

Trust Agreement Located ____________________

Trustees are ____________________

____

The Lawyer or Bank who drew the Trust Agreement is:

Name ____________________

Addr. ____________________

____

Tele. ____________________

Benefit of ____________________

Established On ____________________

Trust Agreement Located ____________________

Trustees are ____________________

____

The Lawyer or Bank who drew the Trust Agreement is:

Name ____________________

Addr. ____________________

____

Tele. ____________________

Benefit of ____________________

Established On ____________________

Trust Agreement Located ____________________

Trustees are ____________________

____

The Lawyer or Bank who drew the Trust Agreement is:

Name ____________________

Addr. ____________________

____

Tele. ____________________

Benefit of ____________________

Established On ____________________

Trust Agreement Located ____________________

Trustees are ____________________

____

The Lawyer or Bank who drew the Trust Agreement is:

Name ____________________

Addr. ____________________

____

Tele. ____________________

Additional Data from Page _____

TRUST FUNDS

☐ I, ____________________________, am a Beneficiary under a Trust established by:
____.

☐ I, ____________________________, am a Beneficiary under a Trust established by:
____.

The above Trust documents are located at: ______________________________________
____
____

When I, __________________________, die my heirs are beneficiaries of Trust Funds established by: ____.

When I, __________________________, die my heirs are beneficiaries of Trust Funds established by: ____.

The above documents are located at: ____
____
____

Additional Data from Page _____

ACCOUNT WITH BROKER

MARGIN ACCOUNT RECORD

Account is with:

Brokerage Firm ____________________

Account Executive ____________________

Broker Telephone ____________________

Account is in the Name of: ____________________

Account Number is: ____________________

			Balance	
Trans. Date	**S/B*	*Description of Transaction (Stock Name, Shares, Security, Cost, etc.)*	*Due from Broker*	*Due to Broker*

* S = Sold, B = Bought

Additional Data from Page _____

ACCOUNT WITH BROKER

MARGIN ACCOUNT RECORD

Account is with:

Brokerage Firm ______________________

Account Executive ______________________

Broker Telephone ______________________

Account is in the Name of: ______________________

Account Number is: ______________________

Trans. Date	*S/B	Description of Transaction (Stock Name, Shares, Security, Cost, etc.)	Balance	
			Due from Broker	Due to Broker

* S = Sold, B = Bought

Additional Data from Page ____

ACCOUNT WITH BROKER

MARGIN ACCOUNT RECORD

Account is with:

Brokerage Firm ____________________

Account Executive ____________________

Broker Telephone ____________________

Account is in the Name of: ____________________

Account Number is: ____________________

			Balance	
Trans. Date	**S/B*	*Description of Transaction (Stock Name, Shares, Security, Cost, etc.)*	*Due from Broker*	*Due to Broker*

* S = Sold, B = Bought

Additional Data from Page ______

ACCOUNT WITH BROKER

MARGIN ACCOUNT RECORD

Account is with:

Brokerage Firm ____________________

Account Executive ____________________

Broker Telephone ____________________

Account is in the Name of: ____________________

Account Number is: ____________________

			Balance	
Trans. Date	**S/B*	*Description of Transaction (Stock Name, Shares, Security, Cost, etc.)*	*Due from Broker*	*Due to Broker*

* S = Sold, B = Bought

Additional Data from Page _____

ACCOUNT WITH BROKER

MARGIN ACCOUNT RECORD

Account is with:

Brokerage Firm ____________________________

Account Executive ____________________________

Broker Telephone ____________________________

Account is in the Name of: ____________________________

Account Number is: ____________________________

			Balance	
Trans. Date	**S/B*	*Description of Transaction (Stock Name, Shares, Security, Cost, etc.)*	*Due from Broker*	*Due to Broker*

* S = Sold, B = Bought

Additional Data from Page _____

ACCOUNT WITH BROKER

MARGIN ACCOUNT RECORD

Account is with:

Brokerage Firm ______________________

Account Executive ______________________

Broker Telephone ______________________

Account is in the Name of: ______________________

Account Number is: ______________________

Trans. Date	**S/B*	*Description of Transaction (Stock Name, Shares, Security, Cost, etc.)*	*Balance*	
			Due from Broker	*Due to Broker*

* S = Sold, B = Bought

Additional Data from Page _____

ACCOUNT WITH BROKER

MARGIN ACCOUNT RECORD

Account is with:

Brokerage Firm ______________________________

Account Executive ______________________________

Broker Telephone ______________________________

Account is in the Name of: ______________________________

Account Number is: ______________________________

			Balance	
Trans. Date	**S/B*	*Description of Transaction (Stock Name, Shares, Security, Cost, etc.)*	*Due from Broker*	*Due to Broker*

* S = Sold, B = Bought

Additional Data from Page _____

ACCOUNT WITH BROKER

MARGIN ACCOUNT RECORD

Account is with:

Brokerage Firm ________________________________

Account Executive ________________________________

Broker Telephone ________________________________

Account is in the Name of: ________________________________

Account Number is: ________________________________

			Balance	
Trans. Date	**S/B*	*Description of Transaction (Stock Name, Shares, Security, Cost, etc.)*	*Due from Broker*	*Due to Broker*

* S = Sold, B = Bought

Additional Data from Page _____

ACCOUNT WITH BROKER

MARGIN ACCOUNT RECORD

Account is with:

Brokerage Firm ____________________

Account Executive ____________________

Broker Telephone ____________________

Account is in the Name of: ____________________

Account Number is: ____________________

			Balance	
Trans. Date	**S/B*	*Description of Transaction (Stock Name, Shares, Security, Cost, etc.)*	*Due from Broker*	*Due to Broker*

* S = Sold, B = Bought

Additional Data from Page _____

ACCOUNT WITH BROKER

MARGIN ACCOUNT RECORD

Account is with:

Brokerage Firm ______________________

Account Executive ______________________

Broker Telephone ______________________

Account is in the Name of: ______________________

Account Number is: ______________________

Trans. Date	**S/B*	*Description of Transaction (Stock Name, Shares, Security, Cost, etc.)*	*Balance*	
			Due from Broker	*Due to Broker*

* S = Sold, B = Bought

Additional Data from Page _____

ACCOUNT WITH BROKER

MARGIN ACCOUNT RECORD

Account is with:

Brokerage Firm ____________________

Account Executive ____________________

Broker Telephone ____________________

Account is in the Name of: ____________________

Account Number is: ____________________

Trans. Date	**S/B*	*Description of Transaction (Stock Name, Shares, Security, Cost, etc.)*	*Balance*	
			Due from Broker	*Due to Broker*

* S = Sold, B = Bought

Additional Data from Page _____

ACCOUNT WITH BROKER

CASH ACCOUNT RECORD

Account is with:

Brokerage Firm ______________________________

Account Executive ______________________________

Broker Telephone ______________________________

Account is in the Name of: ______________________________

Account Number is: ______________________________

			Balance	
Trans. Date	**S/B*	*Description of Transaction (Stock Name, Shares, Security, Cost, etc.)*	*Due from Broker*	*Due to Broker*

* S = Sold, B = Bought

Additional Data from Page _____

ACCOUNT WITH BROKER

CASH ACCOUNT RECORD

Account is with:

Brokerage Firm ______________________________

Account Executive ______________________________

Broker Telephone ______________________________

Account is in the Name of: ______________________________

Account Number is: ______________________________

Trans. Date	**S/B*	*Description of Transaction (Stock Name, Shares, Security, Cost, etc.)*	*Balance*	
			Due from Broker	*Due to Broker*

* S = Sold, B = Bought

Additional Data from Page _____

ACCOUNT WITH BROKER

CASH ACCOUNT RECORD

Account is with:

Brokerage Firm ______________________

Account Executive ______________________

Broker Telephone ______________________

Account is in the Name of: ______________________

Account Number is: ______________________

			Balance	
Trans. Date	**S/B*	*Description of Transaction (Stock Name, Shares, Security, Cost, etc.)*	*Due from Broker*	*Due to Broker*

* S = Sold, B = Bought

Additional Data from Page ____

ACCOUNT WITH BROKER

CASH ACCOUNT RECORD

Account is with:

Brokerage Firm ______________________________

Account Executive ______________________________

Broker Telephone ______________________________

Account is in the Name of: ______________________________

Account Number is: ______________________________

			Balance	
Trans. Date	**S/B*	*Description of Transaction (Stock Name, Shares, Security, Cost, etc.)*	*Due from Broker*	*Due to Broker*

* S = Sold, B = Bought

Additional Data from Page _____

ACCOUNT WITH BROKER

CASH ACCOUNT RECORD

Account is with:

Brokerage Firm ______________________

Account Executive ______________________

Broker Telephone ______________________

Account is in the Name of: ______________________

Account Number is: ______________________

Trans. Date	**S/B*	*Description of Transaction (Stock Name, Shares, Security, Cost, etc.)*	*Balance*	
			Due from Broker	*Due to Broker*

* S = Sold, B = Bought

Additional Data from Page ______

ACCOUNT WITH BROKER

CASH ACCOUNT RECORD

Account is with:

Brokerage Firm ______________________

Account Executive ______________________

Broker Telephone ______________________

Account is in the Name of: ______________________

Account Number is: ______________________

Trans. Date	**S/B*	*Description of Transaction (Stock Name, Shares, Security, Cost, etc.)*	*Balance*	
			Due from Broker	*Due to Broker*

* S = Sold, B = Bought

Additional Data from Page _____

ACCOUNT WITH BROKER

CASH ACCOUNT RECORD

Account is with:

Brokerage Firm ______________________

Account Executive ______________________

Broker Telephone ______________________

Account is in the Name of: ______________________

Account Number is: ______________________

Trans. Date	**S/B*	*Description of Transaction (Stock Name, Shares, Security, Cost, etc.)*	*Balance*	
			Due from Broker	*Due to Broker*

* S = Sold, B = Bought

Additional Data from Page ____

ACCOUNT WITH BROKER

CASH ACCOUNT RECORD

Account is with:

Brokerage Firm ____________________

Account Executive ____________________

Broker Telephone ____________________

Account is in the Name of: ____________________

Account Number is: ____________________

			Balance	
Trans. Date	**S/B*	*Description of Transaction (Stock Name, Shares, Security, Cost, etc.)*	*Due from Broker*	*Due to Broker*

* S = Sold, B = Bought

Additional Data from Page _____

SECURITIES BOUGHT AND SOLD

Security Name ________________
Date Bought ______
Number of Shares ______
Total Cost .... $

Date Sold ______
Number of Shares ______
Net Proceeds .... $
Gain or (Loss)............... $ ________

Additional Information, enter below
(Stock Splits, Special Distributions, etc.)

Security Name ________________
Date Bought ______
Number of Shares ______
Total Cost .... $

Date Sold ______
Number of Shares ______
Net Proceeds .... $
Gain or (Loss)............... $ ________

Additional Information, enter below
(Stock Splits, Special Distributions, etc.)

Security Name ________________
Date Bought ______
Number of Shares ______
Total Cost .... $

Date Sold ______
Number of Shares ______
Net Proceeds .... $
Gain or (Loss)............... $ ________

Additional Information, enter below
(Stock Splits, Special Distributions, etc.)

Security Name ________________
Date Bought ______
Number of Shares ______
Total Cost .... $

Date Sold ______
Number of Shares ______
Net Proceeds .... $
Gain or (Loss)............... $ ________

Additional Information, enter below
(Stock Splits, Special Distributions, etc.)

Additional Data from Page _____

SECURITIES BOUGHT AND SOLD

Security Name ______________
Date Bought _____
Number of Shares _____
Total Cost .... $
Date Sold _____
Number of Shares _____
Net Proceeds .... $
Gain or (Loss).............. $
Additional Information, enter below
(Stock Splits, Special Distributions, etc.)

Security Name ______________
Date Bought _____
Number of Shares _____
Total Cost .... $
Date Sold _____
Number of Shares _____
Net Proceeds .... $
Gain or (Loss).............. $
Additional Information, enter below
(Stock Splits, Special Distributions, etc.)

Security Name ______________
Date Bought _____
Number of Shares _____
Total Cost .... $
Date Sold _____
Number of Shares _____
Net Proceeds .... $
Gain or (Loss).............. $
Additional Information, enter below
(Stock Splits, Special Distributions, etc.)

Security Name ______________
Date Bought _____
Number of Shares _____
Total Cost .... $
Date Sold _____
Number of Shares _____
Net Proceeds .... $
Gain or (Loss).............. $
Additional Information, enter below
(Stock Splits, Special Distributions, etc.)

Additional Data from Page _____

SECURITIES BOUGHT AND SOLD

Security Name ______________
Date Bought _____
Number of Shares _____
Total Cost .... $

Date Sold _____
Number of Shares _____
Net Proceeds .... $
Gain or (Loss)............... $ __________

Additional Information, enter below
(Stock Splits, Special Distributions, etc.)

Security Name ______________
Date Bought _____
Number of Shares _____
Total Cost .... $

Date Sold _____
Number of Shares _____
Net Proceeds .... $
Gain or (Loss)............... $ __________

Additional Information, enter below
(Stock Splits, Special Distributions, etc.)

Security Name ______________
Date Bought _____
Number of Shares _____
Total Cost .... $

Date Sold _____
Number of Shares _____
Net Proceeds .... $
Gain or (Loss)............... $ __________

Additional Information, enter below
(Stock Splits, Special Distributions, etc.)

Security Name ______________
Date Bought _____
Number of Shares _____
Total Cost .... $

Date Sold _____
Number of Shares _____
Net Proceeds .... $
Gain or (Loss)............... $ __________

Additional Information, enter below
(Stock Splits, Special Distributions, etc.)

Additional Data from Page _____

SECURITIES BOUGHT AND SOLD

Security Name ______________

Date Bought ______

Number of Shares ______

Total Cost .... $

Date Sold ______

Number of Shares ______

Net Proceeds .... $

Gain or (Loss).............. $ ________

Additional Information, enter below
(Stock Splits, Special Distributions, etc.)

____

____

____

____

____

Security Name ______________

Date Bought ______

Number of Shares ______

Total Cost .... $

Date Sold ______

Number of Shares ______

Net Proceeds .... $

Gain or (Loss).............. $ ________

Additional Information, enter below
(Stock Splits, Special Distributions, etc.)

____

____

____

____

____

Security Name ______________

Date Bought ______

Number of Shares ______

Total Cost .... $

Date Sold ______

Number of Shares ______

Net Proceeds .... $

Gain or (Loss).............. $ ________

Additional Information, enter below
(Stock Splits, Special Distributions, etc.)

____

____

____

____

____

Security Name ______________

Date Bought ______

Number of Shares ______

Total Cost .... $

Date Sold ______

Number of Shares ______

Net Proceeds .... $

Gain or (Loss).............. $ ________

Additional Information, enter below
(Stock Splits, Special Distributions, etc.)

____

____

____

____

____

Additional Data from Page ______

SECURITIES BOUGHT AND SOLD

Security Name ____________
Date Bought ____
Number of Shares ____
Total Cost .... $ ______

Date Sold ____
Number of Shares ____
Net Proceeds .... $ ______
Gain or (Loss).............. $ ______

Additional Information, enter below
(Stock Splits, Special Distributions, etc.)

Security Name ____________
Date Bought ____
Number of Shares ____
Total Cost .... $ ______

Date Sold ____
Number of Shares ____
Net Proceeds .... $ ______
Gain or (Loss).............. $ ______

Additional Information, enter below
(Stock Splits, Special Distributions, etc.)

Security Name ____________
Date Bought ____
Number of Shares ____
Total Cost .... $ ______

Date Sold ____
Number of Shares ____
Net Proceeds .... $ ______
Gain or (Loss).............. $ ______

Additional Information, enter below
(Stock Splits, Special Distributions, etc.)

Security Name ____________
Date Bought ____
Number of Shares ____
Total Cost .... $ ______

Date Sold ____
Number of Shares ____
Net Proceeds .... $ ______
Gain or (Loss).............. $ ______

Additional Information, enter below
(Stock Splits, Special Distributions, etc.)

Additional Data from Page _____

SECURITIES BOUGHT AND SOLD

Security Name ______________
Date Bought _____
Number of Shares _____
Total Cost .... $

Date Sold _____
Number of Shares _____
Net Proceeds .... $
Gain or (Loss)............... $ ________

Additional Information, enter below
(Stock Splits, Special Distributions, etc.)

Security Name ______________
Date Bought _____
Number of Shares _____
Total Cost .... $

Date Sold _____
Number of Shares _____
Net Proceeds .... $
Gain or (Loss)............... $ ________

Additional Information, enter below
(Stock Splits, Special Distributions, etc.)

Security Name ______________
Date Bought _____
Number of Shares _____
Total Cost .... $

Date Sold _____
Number of Shares _____
Net Proceeds .... $
Gain or (Loss)............... $ ________

Additional Information, enter below
(Stock Splits, Special Distributions, etc.)

Security Name ______________
Date Bought _____
Number of Shares _____
Total Cost .... $

Date Sold _____
Number of Shares _____
Net Proceeds .... $
Gain or (Loss)............... $ ________

Additional Information, enter below
(Stock Splits, Special Distributions, etc.)

Additional Data from Page _____

SECURITIES BOUGHT AND SOLD

Security Name ____________
Date Bought ______
Number of Shares ______
Total Cost .... $

Date Sold ______
Number of Shares ______
Net Proceeds .... $
Gain or (Loss).............. $

Additional Information, enter below
(Stock Splits, Special Distributions, etc.)

Security Name ____________
Date Bought ______
Number of Shares ______
Total Cost .... $

Date Sold ______
Number of Shares ______
Net Proceeds .... $
Gain or (Loss).............. $

Additional Information, enter below
(Stock Splits, Special Distributions, etc.)

Security Name ____________
Date Bought ______
Number of Shares ______
Total Cost .... $

Date Sold ______
Number of Shares ______
Net Proceeds .... $
Gain or (Loss).............. $

Additional Information, enter below
(Stock Splits, Special Distributions, etc.)

Security Name ____________
Date Bought ______
Number of Shares ______
Total Cost .... $

Date Sold ______
Number of Shares ______
Net Proceeds .... $
Gain or (Loss).............. $

Additional Information, enter below
(Stock Splits, Special Distributions, etc.)

Additional Data from Page _____

SECURITIES BOUGHT AND SOLD

Security Name ______________
Date Bought ______
Number of Shares ______
Total Cost .... $

Date Sold ______
Number of Shares ______
Net Proceeds .... $
Gain or (Loss).............. $ ______

Additional Information, enter below
(Stock Splits, Special Distributions, etc.)

Security Name ______________
Date Bought ______
Number of Shares ______
Total Cost .... $

Date Sold ______
Number of Shares ______
Net Proceeds .... $
Gain or (Loss).............. $ ______

Additional Information, enter below
(Stock Splits, Special Distributions, etc.)

Security Name ______________
Date Bought ______
Number of Shares ______
Total Cost .... $

Date Sold ______
Number of Shares ______
Net Proceeds .... $
Gain or (Loss).............. $ ______

Additional Information, enter below
(Stock Splits, Special Distributions, etc.)

Security Name ______________
Date Bought ______
Number of Shares ______
Total Cost .... $

Date Sold ______
Number of Shares ______
Net Proceeds .... $
Gain or (Loss).............. $ ______

Additional Information, enter below
(Stock Splits, Special Distributions, etc.)

Additional Data from Page _____

SECURITIES BOUGHT AND SOLD

Security Name __________
Date Bought ______
Number of Shares ______
Total Cost .... $

Date Sold ______
Number of Shares ______
Net Proceeds .... $
Gain or (Loss).............. $

Additional Information, enter below
(Stock Splits, Special Distributions, etc.)

Security Name __________
Date Bought ______
Number of Shares ______
Total Cost .... $

Date Sold ______
Number of Shares ______
Net Proceeds .... $
Gain or (Loss).............. $

Additional Information, enter below
(Stock Splits, Special Distributions, etc.)

Security Name __________
Date Bought ______
Number of Shares ______
Total Cost .... $

Date Sold ______
Number of Shares ______
Net Proceeds .... $
Gain or (Loss).............. $

Additional Information, enter below
(Stock Splits, Special Distributions, etc.)

Security Name __________
Date Bought ______
Number of Shares ______
Total Cost .... $

Date Sold ______
Number of Shares ______
Net Proceeds .... $
Gain or (Loss).............. $

Additional Information, enter below
(Stock Splits, Special Distributions, etc.)

Additional Data from Page _____

SECURITIES BOUGHT AND SOLD

Security Name ______________
Date Bought ______
Number of Shares ______
Total Cost .... $

Date Sold ______
Number of Shares ______
Net Proceeds .... $
Gain or (Loss).............. $

Additional Information, enter below
(Stock Splits, Special Distributions, etc.)

Security Name ______________
Date Bought ______
Number of Shares ______
Total Cost .... $

Date Sold ______
Number of Shares ______
Net Proceeds .... $
Gain or (Loss).............. $

Additional Information, enter below
(Stock Splits, Special Distributions, etc.)

Security Name ______________
Date Bought ______
Number of Shares ______
Total Cost .... $

Date Sold ______
Number of Shares ______
Net Proceeds .... $
Gain or (Loss).............. $

Additional Information, enter below
(Stock Splits, Special Distributions, etc.)

Security Name ______________
Date Bought ______
Number of Shares ______
Total Cost .... $

Date Sold ______
Number of Shares ______
Net Proceeds .... $
Gain or (Loss).............. $

Additional Information, enter below
(Stock Splits, Special Distributions, etc.)

Additional Data from Page _____

DIVIDENDS AND INTEREST INCOME

Name of Security						
Due Dates →						
Amount Expected→	$	$	$	$	$	$
	Amount Rec'd / Date Rec'd	*Amount Rec'd / Date Rec'd*	*Amount Rec'd / Date Rec'd*	*Amount Rec'd / Date Rec'd*	*Amount Rec'd / Date Rec'd*	*Amount Rec'd / Date Rec'd*

Enter below any additional or special dividends, distributions, etc.:

Name of Security	*Date*	*Description of Income*	*Amount $*
			$
			$
			$
			$
			$
			$

Additional Data from Page _____

DIVIDENDS AND INTEREST INCOME

Name of Security						
Due Dates →						
Amount Expected→	$	$	$	$	$	$
	Amount Rec'd / Date Rec'd	*Amount Rec'd / Date Rec'd*	*Amount Rec'd / Date Rec'd*	*Amount Rec'd / Date Rec'd*	*Amount Rec'd / Date Rec'd*	*Amount Rec'd / Date Rec'd*

Enter below any additional or special dividends, distributions, etc.:

Name of Security	*Date*	*Description of Income*	*Amount $*
			$
			$
			$
			$
			$
			$

Additional Data from Page _____

DIVIDENDS AND INTEREST INCOME

Name of Security						
Due Dates →						
Amount Expected→	$	$	$	$	$	$
	Amount Rec'd / Date Rec'd	*Amount Rec'd / Date Rec'd*	*Amount Rec'd / Date Rec'd*	*Amount Rec'd / Date Rec'd*	*Amount Rec'd / Date Rec'd*	*Amount Rec'd / Date Rec'd*

Enter below any additional or special dividends, distributions, etc.:

Name of Security	*Date*	*Description of Income*	*Amount $*
			$
			$
			$
			$
			$
			$

Additional Data from Page _____

DIVIDENDS AND INTEREST INCOME

Name of Security						
Due Dates →						
Amount Expected→	$	$	$	$	$	$
	Amount Rec'd / Date Rec'd	*Amount Rec'd / Date Rec'd*	*Amount Rec'd / Date Rec'd*	*Amount Rec'd / Date Rec'd*	*Amount Rec'd / Date Rec'd*	*Amount Rec'd / Date Rec'd*

Enter below any additional or special dividends, distributions, etc.:

Name of Security	*Date*	*Description of Income*	*Amount $*
			$
			$
			$
			$
			$
			$

Additional Data from Page _____

DIVIDENDS AND INTEREST INCOME

Name of Security						
Due Dates →						
Amount Expected→	$	$	$	$	$	$
	Amount Rec'd / Date Rec'd	*Amount Rec'd / Date Rec'd*	*Amount Rec'd / Date Rec'd*	*Amount Rec'd / Date Rec'd*	*Amount Rec'd / Date Rec'd*	*Amount Rec'd / Date Rec'd*

Enter below any additional or special dividends, distributions, etc.:

Name of Security	*Date*	*Description of Income*	*Amount $*
			$
			$
			$
			$
			$
			$

Additional Data from Page ____

DIVIDENDS AND INTEREST INCOME

Name of Security						
Due Dates →						
Amount Expected→	$	$	$	$	$	$
	Amount Rec'd / Date Rec'd	*Amount Rec'd / Date Rec'd*	*Amount Rec'd / Date Rec'd*	*Amount Rec'd / Date Rec'd*	*Amount Rec'd / Date Rec'd*	*Amount Rec'd / Date Rec'd*

Enter below any additional or special dividends, distributions, etc.:

Name of Security	*Date*	*Description of Income*	*Amount $*
			$
			$
			$
			$
			$
			$

Additional Data from Page _____

MUTUAL FUNDS

Mutual Fund Name ____________________

Original Purchase Date ____________________

Number of Shares ____________________

Original Cost of Shares ____________________

Account Number is ____________________

Other Specifics: ____________________
(Leverage Funding, etc.) ____________________

Enter Below Data as Account Status Notices are Received.

Date	*Income Div.*		*Capital Gain Distribution*	*Number of Shares Received*	*Total Number of Shares Held*	*Value Per Share*	*Total Value of Shares*
	Qual. / Non Qual.	*Total Rec'd*					
							$
							$
							$
							$
							$
							$
							$
							$
							$
							$
							$
							$
							$
							$

Additional Data from Page ____

MUTUAL FUNDS

Mutual Fund Name ____________________

Original Purchase Date ____________________

Number of Shares ____________________

Original Cost of Shares ____________________

Account Number is ____________________

Other Specifics: ____________________
(Leverage Funding, etc.) ____________________

Enter Below Data as Account Status Notices are Received.

Date	*Income Div.* Qual. / Non Qual.	*Income Div.* Total Rec'd	*Capital Gain Distribution*	*Number of Shares Received*	*Total Number of Shares Held*	*Value Per Share*	*Total Value of Shares*
							$
							$
							$
							$
							$
							$
							$
							$
							$
							$
							$
							$
							$
							$

Additional Data from Page _____

MUTUAL FUNDS

Mutual Fund Name ______________________

Original Purchase Date ______________________

Number of Shares ______________________

Original Cost of Shares ______________________

Account Number is ______________________

Other Specifics: ______________________
(Leverage Funding, etc.) ______________________

Enter Below Data as Account Status Notices are Received.

Date	*Income Div.*		*Capital Gain Distribution*	*Number of Shares Received*	*Total Number of Shares Held*	*Value Per Share*	*Total Value of Shares*
	Qual. / Non Qual.	*Total Rec'd*					
							$
							$
							$
							$
							$
							$
							$
							$
							$
							$
							$
							$
							$
							$

Additional Data from Page _____

MUTUAL FUNDS

Mutual Fund Name ______________________

Original Purchase Date ______________________

Number of Shares ______________________

Original Cost of Shares ______________________

Account Number is ______________________

Other Specifics: ______________________
(Leverage Funding, etc.) ______________________

Enter Below Data as Account Status Notices are Received.

Date	*Income Div.*		*Capital Gain Distribution*	*Number of Shares Received*	*Total Number of Shares Held*	*Value Per Share*	*Total Value of Shares*
	Qual. / Non Qual.	*Total Rec'd*					
							$
							$
							$
							$
							$
							$
							$
							$
							$
							$
							$
							$
							$
							$

Additional Data from Page ____

MUTUAL FUNDS

Mutual Fund Name ______________________

Original Purchase Date ______________________

Number of Shares ______________________

Original Cost of Shares ______________________

Account Number is ______________________

Other Specifics: ______________________
(Leverage Funding, etc.) ______________________

Enter Below Data as Account Status Notices are Received.

Date	*Income Div.* Qual. / Non Qual.	*Total Rec'd*	*Capital Gain Distribution*	*Number of Shares Received*	*Total Number of Shares Held*	*Value Per Share*	*Total Value of Shares*
							$
							$
							$
							$
							$
							$
							$
							$
							$
							$
							$
							$
							$
							$

Additional Data from Page _____

SAVINGS BONDS

Date Purch./Rec'd	*Series Number*	*Owner/Beneficiary*	*Maturity Date*	*Maturity Value*	

Additional Data from Page ______

SAVINGS BONDS

Date Purch./Rec'd	*Series Number*	*Owner/Beneficiary*	*Maturity Date*	*Maturity Value*	

Additional Data from Page _____

SAVINGS BONDS

Date Purch./Rec'd	*Series Number*	*Owner/Beneficiary*	*Maturity Date*	*Maturity Value*	

Additional Data from Page _____

SAVINGS BONDS

Date Purch./Rec'd	*Series Number*	*Owner/Beneficiary*	*Maturity Date*	*Maturity Value*	

Additional Data from Page _____

PROPERTY SAFEKEEPING

FAMILY PROPERTY SAFEKEEPING—SAFE DEPOSIT BOXES

SAFE DEPOSIT BOX NUMBER ☐

This Safe Deposit Box is located at:

Bank ____________ Contact ____________

Branch ____________ Title ____________

Addr. ____________ Tele. ____________

____

This Safe Deposit Box is: ☐ in the name of ____________

☐ joint name with ____________

It requires ________ signatures to open the box.

The following people have access to this box:

Name ____________ Name ____________

Addr. ____________ Addr. ____________

____________ ____________

Tele. ____________ Tele. ____________

Possesses a KEY ☐ YES ☐ NO Possesses a KEY ☐ YES ☐ NO

I have the following property, owned BY OTHERS, in the above Safe Deposit Box:

Owner	*Type of Property*

A KEY TO THIS SAFE DEPOSIT BOX IS LOCATED AT

____

____

____

Additional Data from Page _____

PROPERTY SAFEKEEPING

FAMILY PROPERTY SAFEKEEPING—SAFE DEPOSIT BOXES

SAFE DEPOSIT BOX NUMBER ☐

The following is a SAFE DEPOSIT BOX INVENTORY for the above box.
CHECK (✓) items kept in the above:

- ☐ Will
- ☐ Birth Certificates
- ☐ Death Certificates
- ☐ Cemetery Deeds
- ☐ Military Discharge Papers
- ☐ Professional Licenses
- ☐ Employment Contract
- ☐ Apartment Lease
- ☐ Credit Union Savings Book
- ☐ Savings Bank Passbooks
- ☐ Trust Agreement
- ☐ Title on Property ______
- ☐ Title on Property ______
- ☐ Title on Property ______
- ☐ Bill of Sales for ______
- ☐ Addendum/Codicil to Will
- ☐ Divorce/Separation Agreement
- ☐ Marriage Certificates
- ☐ Citizenship Papers
- ☐ Keys to Personal Safe
- ☐ Pension Plan/IRA Contract
- ☐ Keys to Vacation Home
- ☐ Certificates of Doing Business
- ☐ Passports
- ☐ Diplomas
- ☐ Auto Title (make) ______
- ☐ Auto Title (make) ______
- ☐ Boat Title (make) ______
- ☐ Truck Title (make) ______

Other ______

REAL ESTATE (Residence) related items:

- ☐ Deed
- ☐ Surveys
- ☐ Closing Statement
- ☐ Copy of Mortgage
- ☐ Title Insurance Policy
- ☐ Title Abstract
- ☐ Insurance Policies (Homeowners)
- ☐ Tax Receipts
- ☐ Leases
- ☐ Other ______

INSURANCE POLICIES:

Type	*Insured*	*Policy Company and Number*

Additional Data from Page ____

PROPERTY SAFEKEEPING

FAMILY PROPERTY SAFEKEEPING – SAFE DEPOSIT BOXES

SAFE DEPOSIT BOX NUMBER ☐

SAFE DEPOSIT BOX INVENTORY (continued)
CHECK (✓) those items applicable:

☐ Partnership Agreement for ______________________

☐ Partnership Agreement for ______________________

☐ Stockholder's Agreement for ______________________

☐ Stockholder's Agreement for ______________________

The following JEWELRY is kept in the above mentioned:

Description	*Original Cost*	*Jewelry Invoice is Located at:*
	$	
	$	
	$	
	$	
	$	

OTHER ITEMS IN SAFE DEPOSIT BOX

Additional Data from Page _____

PROPERTY SAFEKEEPING

FAMILY PROPERTY SAFEKEEPING—PERSONAL SAFE

My PERSONAL SAFE is located at:

____

____

The (COMBINATION/KEYS) to my SAFE is located at or held by:

____

____

There are ______ sets of KEYS to my safe, and the following people possess a set of these keys.

Name	______________	Name	______________
Addr.	______________	Addr.	______________
	______________		______________
Tele.	______________	Tele.	______________

I have the following property, OWNED BY OTHERS, in my personal safe:

Owner	*Type of Property*

Additional Data from Page _____

PROPERTY SAFEKEEPING

FAMILY PROPERTY SAFEKEEPING—PERSONAL SAFE

The following is a PERSONAL SAFE INVENTORY of my safe located at:

____

CHECK (✔) items kept in the above:

- ☐ Will
- ☐ Birth Certificates
- ☐ Death Certificates
- ☐ Cemetery Deeds
- ☐ Military Discharge Papers
- ☐ Professional Licenses
- ☐ Employment Contract
- ☐ Apartment Lease
- ☐ Credit Union Savings Book
- ☐ Savings Bank Passbooks
- ☐ Trust Agreement
- ☐ Title on Property ____________
- ☐ Title on Property ____________
- ☐ Title on Property ____________
- ☐ Bill of Sales for ____________
- ☐ Addendum/Codicil to Will
- ☐ Divorce/Separation Agreement
- ☐ Marriage Certificates
- ☐ Citizenship Papers
- ☐ Keys to Personal Safe
- ☐ Pension Plan/IRA Contract
- ☐ Keys to Vacation Home
- ☐ Certificates of Doing Business
- ☐ Passports
- ☐ Diplomas
- ☐ Auto Title (make) ____________
- ☐ Auto Title (make) ____________
- ☐ Boat Title (make) ____________
- ☐ Truck Title (make) ____________
- ☐ Other ____________

REAL ESTATE (Residence) related items:

- ☐ Deed
- ☐ Surveys
- ☐ Closing Statement
- ☐ Copy of Mortgage
- ☐ Title Insurance Policy
- ☐ Title Abstract
- ☐ Insurance Policies (Homeowners)
- ☐ Tax Receipts
- ☐ Leases
- ☐ Other ____________

INSURANCE POLICIES:

Type	*Insured*	*Policy Company and Number*
Life	____________	____________
Life	____________	____________
Life	____________	____________
Life	____________	____________
Life	____________	____________
Auto	____________	____________
____________	____________	____________
____________	____________	____________

Additional Data from Page _____

PROPERTY SAFEKEEPING

FAMILY PROPERTY SAFEKEEPING—PERSONAL SAFE

The following is a continuation of my PERSONAL SAFE INVENTORY.

The safe is located at: ______________________________

CHECK (✔) those items applicable:

☐ Partnership Agreement for ______________________________

☐ Partnership Agreement for ______________________________

☐ Stockholder's Agreement for ______________________________

☐ Stockholder's Agreement for ______________________________

The following JEWELRY is kept in the above mentioned:

Description	*Original Cost*	*Jewelry Invoice is Located at:*
	$	
	$	
	$	
	$	
	$	
	$	

OTHER ITEMS IN PERSONAL SAFE

Additional Data from Page _____

PROPERTY SAFEKEEPING

FAMILY PROPERTY SAFEKEEPING – HELD/SHARED BY OTHERS

Family property in the custody of others:

Held By	*Type of Property*	*% Ownership*

Stocks held by others:

☐ See Latest Statements from Brokers

☐ Jointly (Other than Spouse)

☐ As Security, Held by

☐ In Trust, Name of Trust is

☐ By Executor under a Will

☐ Other

The following important papers for safekeeping purposes are at:

Held By	*Description of Property*

Additional Data from Page ______

MAJOR PURCHASES AND POSSESSIONS

Acq. *Date*	*Description and Ser. #*	*Purchased from* *Gifted by*	*Cost* *Assessed Val.*	*Warranty and* *other info.*

Additional Data from Page _____

MAJOR PURCHASES AND POSSESSIONS

Acq. *Date*	*Description and Ser. #*	*Purchased from* *Gifted by*	*Cost* *Assessed Val.*	*Warranty and* *other info.*

Additional Data from Page ____

MAJOR PURCHASES AND POSSESSIONS

Acq. *Date*	*Description and Ser. #*	*Purchased from* *Gifted by*	*Cost* *Assessed Val.*	*Warranty and* *other info.*

Additional Data from Page _____

MAJOR PURCHASES AND POSSESSIONS

Acq. / Date	*Description and Ser. #*	*Purchased from / Gifted by*	*Cost / Assessed Val.*	*Warranty and other info.*

Additional Data from Page _____

MAJOR PURCHASES AND POSSESSIONS

Acq. / Date	Description and Ser. #	Purchased from / Gifted by	Cost / Assessed Val.	Warranty and / other info.

Additional Data from Page _____

FAMILY REAL ESTATE

☐ Residence ADDRESS: ______________________

☐ Cemetery Plot ______________________

☐ Other __________ ______________________

BLOCK NO. ______ SECTION NO. ______ PROPERTY SIZE ____ X ____

ASSESSMENT AMOUNT $__________ ASSESSMENT DATE ________

OWNERSHIP TITLE is held in: ☐ (HUSBAND/WIFE) only *OR*

☐ JOINT OWNERSHIP with: ______________________

____

____

MORTGAGE ☐ NO ☐ YES, held by: ______________________

Original Amount $ ____________ Addr. ______________________

Mortgage Number ____________ ______________________

Mortgage Interest ____________% Term ______________________YRS.

Number of POINTS paid for and how much: ____________$____________

Bal. Due on MORTGAGE at (Date): ____________ AMOUNT—$ ____________

SECOND MORTGAGE ☐ NO ☐ YES, held by: ______________________

Mortgage Amount $ ____________ Addr. ______________________

Mortgage Interest ____________% ______________________

Date Mortgage Made ____________ Term ______________________YRS.

Bal. Due on MORTGAGE at (Date): ____________ AMOUNT—$ ____________

The following CHECKED (✔) documents are located at:

____

Safe Deposit Box # ______________________

____________ ______________________

☐ DEED

☐ SURVEYS

☐ LEASES

☐ TAX RECEIPTS

☐ TITLE ABSTRACT

☐ TERMITE REPORT

☐ Other ______________________

☐ Other ______________________

☐ CLOSING STATEMENT

☐ COPY OF MORTGAGE

☐ TITLE INSURANCE POLICY

☐ INSURANCE POLICIES

☐ BUILDING COST FIGURES

☐ ENGINEERING REPORT

☐ Other ______________________

☐ Other ______________________

Additional Data from Page _____

FAMILY REAL ESTATE

... FINAL COST of HOUSE as per CLOSING STATEMENT $ ____________

Add: Continuing Home Improvements: (SAVE ALL BILLS)*

DRIVEWAY	$______	NEW LAWN	$______
NEW ROOFING	$______	NEW TREES	$______
NEW STAIRWAYS	$______	NEW PORCH	$______
NEW DOORS	$______	NEW KITCHEN	$______
NEW WINDOWS	$______	ADDED ROOM	$______
SCREENS/STORMS	$______	OTHER (______)	$______
AIR CONDITIONING	$______	(______)	$______
BUILT-IN FANS	$______	(______)	$______
SWIMMING POOL	$______	(______)	$______
NEW STRUCTURING	$______	(______)	$______

REAL ESTATE LAWYER IS:

Name ____________

Firm ____________

Addr. ____________

____

Tele. ____________

REAL ESTATE BROKER IS:

Name ____________

Firm ____________

Addr. ____________

____

Tele. ____________

GENERAL INSURANCE BROKER IS:

Name ____________

Firm ____________

Addr. ____________

____

Tele. ____________

PROPERTY MANAGED BY:

Super ____________

Firm ____________

Addr. ____________

____

Tele. ____________

OTHER INFORMATION

____

____

____

____

____

Additional Data from Page _____

FAMILY REAL ESTATE

☐ Residence ADDRESS: ____________________
☐ Cemetery Plot ____________________
☐ Other ________ ____________________

BLOCK NO. ______ SECTION NO. ______ PROPERTY SIZE ___ X ___
ASSESSMENT AMOUNT $________ ASSESSMENT DATE ________

OWNERSHIP TITLE is held in: ☐ (HUSBAND/WIFE) only *OR*
☐ JOINT OWNERSHIP with: ____________________
____
____

MORTGAGE ☐ NO ☐ YES, held by: ____________________
Original Amount $ ____________ Addr. ____________________
Mortgage Number ____________ ____________________
Mortgage Interest ____________% Term ____________________YRS.
Number of POINTS paid for and how much: ________$________
Bal. Due on MORTGAGE at (Date): ____________ AMOUNT–$________

SECOND MORTGAGE ☐ NO ☐ YES, held by: ____________________
Mortgage Amount $ ____________ Addr. ____________________
Mortgage Interest ____________% ____________________
Date Mortgage Made ____________ Term ____________________YRS.
Bal. Due on MORTGAGE at (Date): ____________ AMOUNT–$________

The following CHECKED (✔) documents are located at:

____
Safe Deposit Box # ____________________
____________ ____________________

☐ DEED ☐ CLOSING STATEMENT
☐ SURVEYS ☐ COPY OF MORTGAGE
☐ LEASES ☐ TITLE INSURANCE POLICY
☐ TAX RECEIPTS ☐ INSURANCE POLICIES
☐ TITLE ABSTRACT ☐ BUILDING COST FIGURES
☐ TERMITE REPORT ☐ ENGINEERING REPORT
☐ Other ____________ ☐ Other ____________
☐ Other ____________ ☐ Other ____________

Additional Data from Page _____

FAMILY REAL ESTATE

... FINAL COST of HOUSE as per CLOSING STATEMENT $ ______

Add: Continuing Home Improvements: (SAVE ALL BILLS)*

DRIVEWAY	$______	NEW LAWN	$______
NEW ROOFING	$______	NEW TREES	$______
NEW STAIRWAYS	$______	NEW PORCH	$______
NEW DOORS	$______	NEW KITCHEN	$______
NEW WINDOWS	$______	ADDED ROOM	$______
SCREENS/STORMS	$______	OTHER (______)	$______
AIR CONDITIONING	$______	(______)	$______
BUILT-IN FANS	$______	(______)	$______
SWIMMING POOL	$______	(______)	$______
NEW STRUCTURING	$______	(______)	$______

REAL ESTATE LAWYER IS:

Name ______

Firm ______

Addr. ______

______

Tele. ______

REAL ESTATE BROKER IS:

Name ______

Firm ______

Addr. ______

______

Tele. ______

GENERAL INSURANCE BROKER IS:

Name ______

Firm ______

Addr. ______

______

Tele. ______

PROPERTY MANAGED BY:

Super ______

Firm ______

Addr. ______

______

Tele. ______

OTHER INFORMATION

______

______

______

______

______

Additional Data from Page _____

FAMILY REAL ESTATE

☐ Residence ADDRESS: ______________________

☐ Cemetery Plot ______________________

☐ Other __________ ______________________

BLOCK NO. ______ SECTION NO. ______ PROPERTY SIZE ___ X ___

ASSESSMENT AMOUNT $__________ ASSESSMENT DATE __________

OWNERSHIP TITLE is held in: ☐ (HUSBAND/WIFE) only *OR*

☐ JOINT OWNERSHIP with: ______________________

____

____

MORTGAGE ☐ NO ☐ YES, held by: ______________________

Original Amount $ ______________ Addr. ______________________

Mortgage Number ______________ ______________________

Mortgage Interest ______________% Term ______________________ YRS.

Number of POINTS paid for and how much: ______ $ ______

Bal. Due on MORTGAGE at (Date): ______________ AMOUNT – $ ______

SECOND MORTGAGE ☐ NO ☐ YES, held by: ______________________

Mortgage Amount $ ______________ Addr. ______________________

Mortgage Interest ______________% ______________________

Date Mortgage Made ______________ Term ______________________ YRS.

Bal. Due on MORTGAGE at (Date): ______________ AMOUNT – $ ______

The following CHECKED (✔) documents are located at:

____

Safe Deposit Box # ______________________

______________ ______________________

☐ DEED	☐ CLOSING STATEMENT
☐ SURVEYS	☐ COPY OF MORTGAGE
☐ LEASES	☐ TITLE INSURANCE POLICY
☐ TAX RECEIPTS	☐ INSURANCE POLICIES
☐ TITLE ABSTRACT	☐ BUILDING COST FIGURES
☐ TERMITE REPORT	☐ ENGINEERING REPORT
☐ Other ______________	☐ Other ______________
☐ Other ______________	☐ Other ______________

Additional Data from Page ____

FAMILY REAL ESTATE

... FINAL COST of HOUSE as per CLOSING STATEMENT $________

Add: Continuing Home Improvements: (SAVE ALL BILLS)*

DRIVEWAY	$________	NEW LAWN	$________
NEW ROOFING	$________	NEW TREES	$________
NEW STAIRWAYS	$________	NEW PORCH	$________
NEW DOORS	$________	NEW KITCHEN	$________
NEW WINDOWS	$________	ADDED ROOM	$________
SCREENS/STORMS	$________	OTHER (________)	$________
AIR CONDITIONING	$________	(________)	$________
BUILT-IN FANS	$________	(________)	$________
SWIMMING POOL	$________	(________)	$________
NEW STRUCTURING	$________	(________)	$________

REAL ESTATE LAWYER IS:

Name ________________

Firm ________________

Addr. ________________

____

Tele. ________________

REAL ESTATE BROKER IS:

Name ________________

Firm ________________

Addr. ________________

____

Tele. ________________

GENERAL INSURANCE BROKER IS:

Name ________________

Firm ________________

Addr. ________________

____

Tele. ________________

PROPERTY MANAGED BY:

Super ________________

Firm ________________

Addr. ________________

____

Tele. ________________

OTHER INFORMATION

____

____

____

____

____

Additional Data from Page ____

FAMILY RENTAL AND LEASE AGREEMENTS

☐ Apartment Building
☐ Private House
  ☐ Month-to-Month Tenant
  ☐ Lease Agreement (see below)
    ☐ Rent-Controlled Apartment
    ☐ Rent Stabilized Apartment

My Landlord is:
Name ______________________
Firm ______________________
Addr. ______________________
____
Tele. ______________________

My Apartment Superintendent is:
Name ______________________ Tele. (office) ______________________
Apt. # ______________________ Tele. (Apt.) ______________________

The following information pertains to the Lease Agreement:
Term of Lease ______________ Lease Expires on ______________
Monthly Rental $ ______________ Extension Clause for ______________ (yrs.)

The following are SECURITY DEPOSITS, associated with the foregoing premises rented, which have been paid:

Security Deposit	*Amount*	*Date*	*Check No.*	*Returned On*
Lease Agreement	$______	______	______	______
Advance Rent	$______	______	______	______
Telephone	$______	______	______	______
Electric	$______	______	______	______
Gas	$______	______	______	______
Cable T.V.	$______	______	______	______
Water	$______	______	______	______
______	$______	______	______	______
______	$______	______	______	______
______	$______	______	______	______
______	$______	______	______	______

Security Deposit Receipts are located at: ______________________
____
____

Additional Data from Page _____

FAMILY RENTAL AND LEASE AGREEMENTS

☐ Apartment Building
☐ Private House
  ☐ Month-to-Month Tenant
  ☐ Lease Agreement (see below)
    ☐ Rent-Controlled Apartment
    ☐ Rent Stabilized Apartment

My Landlord is:
Name ______________________
Firm ______________________
Addr. ______________________
____
Tele. ______________________

My Apartment Superintendent is:
Name ______________________ Tele. (office) ______________________
Apt. # ______________________ Tele. (Apt.) ______________________

The following information pertains to the Lease Agreement:
Term of Lease ______________ Lease Expires on ______________
Monthly Rental $ ______________ Extension Clause for ______________ (yrs.)

The following are SECURITY DEPOSITS, associated with the foregoing premises rented, which have been paid:

Security Deposit	*Amount*	*Date*	*Check No.*	*Returned On*
Lease Agreement	$______	______	______	______
Advance Rent	$______	______	______	______
Telephone	$______	______	______	______
Electric	$______	______	______	______
Gas	$______	______	______	______
Cable T.V.	$______	______	______	______
Water	$______	______	______	______
______	$______	______	______	______
______	$______	______	______	______
______	$______	______	______	______
______	$______	______	______	______

Security Deposit Receipts are located at: ______________________
____
____

Additional Data from Page ____

FAMILY RENTAL AND LEASE AGREEMENTS

☐ Apartment Building
☐ Private House
  ☐ Month-to-Month Tenant
  ☐ Lease Agreement (see below)
    ☐ Rent-Controlled Apartment
    ☐ Rent Stabilized Apartment

My Landlord is:
Name ____________________
Firm ____________________
Addr. ____________________
____
Tele. ____________________

My Apartment Superintendent is:
Name ____________________ Tele. (office) ____________________
Apt. # ____________________ Tele. (Apt.) ____________________

The following information pertains to the Lease Agreement:
Term of Lease ____________ Lease Expires on ____________
Monthly Rental $ ____________ Extension Clause for ____________ (yrs.)

The following are SECURITY DEPOSITS, associated with the foregoing premises rented, which have been paid:

Security Deposit	*Amount*	*Date*	*Check No.*	*Returned On*
Lease Agreement	$______	______	______	______
Advance Rent	$______	______	______	______
Telephone	$______	______	______	______
Electric	$______	______	______	______
Gas	$______	______	______	______
Cable T.V.	$______	______	______	______
Water	$______	______	______	______
______	$______	______	______	______
______	$______	______	______	______
______	$______	______	______	______
______	$______	______	______	______

Security Deposit Receipts are located at: ____________________
____
____

Additional Data from Page _____

FAMILY PASSPORT INFORMATION

Husband and Wife have JOINT PASSPORT ☐ YES ☐ NO.

	Passport Number	*Date of Issue/Expire*
HUSBAND		
WIFE		
( )		
( )		
( )		
( )		

The above passports are located at:

____

____________________ Safe Deposit Box #

____________________ _______________

INOCULATIONS RECEIVED

Who	*Date*	*Description*

Additional Data from Page ______

INCOME TAX RETURNS

Copies of all personal Income Tax Returns are:

☐ Located at
Addr. ______________________
____
☐ Personal Safe
☐ Safe Deposit Box No. __________
☐ Other Place ______________________

☐ Kept by Accountant
Name ______________________
Addr. ______________________
____
Tele. ______________________

All work sheets and/or evidence in support of tax returns are

☐ Attached to the tax return copies, which are located at the above.

☐ Located at:
____
____

Gift Tax Returns were filed for the following years:

________	________	________
________	________	________
________	________	________

All Gift Tax Returns with worksheets, appraisals, and other supporting evidence are located at:
____
____

My Tax Acct/Lawyer is: ______________________
____

Returns Audited by IRS for these years —		*Disposition of Audit*
	19 ______	______________________
	19 ______	______________________
	19 ______	______________________
	19 ______	______________________

OTHER INFORMATION

____
____
____

Additional Data from Page _____

INCOME TAX RETURNS

Copies of all personal Income Tax Returns are:

☐ Located at
Addr. ______________________
____

☐ Personal Safe
☐ Safe Deposit Box No. __________
☐ Other Place ______________________

☐ Kept by Accountant
Name ______________________
Addr. ______________________
____
Tele. ______________________

All work sheets and/or evidence in support of tax returns are

☐ Attached to the tax return copies, which are located at the above.

☐ Located at:
____
____

Gift Tax Returns were filed for the following years:

________	________	________
________	________	________
________	________	________

All Gift Tax Returns with worksheets, appraisals, and other supporting evidence are located at:
____
____

My Tax Acct/Lawyer is: ______________________
____

Returns Audited by IRS for these years—		*Disposition of Audit*
	19 ____	______________________
	19 ____	______________________
	19 ____	______________________
	19 ____	______________________

OTHER INFORMATION

____
____
____

Additional Data from Page ______

INCOME TAX RETURNS

Copies of all personal Income Tax Returns are:

☐ Located at
Addr. ____________________
____

☐ Personal Safe
☐ Safe Deposit Box No. ________
☐ Other Place ____________________

☐ Kept by Accountant
Name ____________________
Addr. ____________________
____
Tele. ____________________

All work sheets and/or evidence in support of tax returns are

☐ Attached to the tax return copies, which are located at the above.

☐ Located at:
____
____

Gift Tax Returns were filed for the following years:

________	________	________
________	________	________
________	________	________

All Gift Tax Returns with worksheets, appraisals, and other supporting evidence are located at:
____
____

My Tax Acct/Lawyer is: ____________________
____

Returns Audited by IRS for these years—		*Disposition of Audit*
	19	
	19	
	19	
	19	

OTHER INFORMATION

____
____
____

Additional Data from Page _____

INCOME TAX RETURNS

Copies of all personal Income Tax Returns are:

☐ Located at
Addr. ______________________________
____
☐ Personal Safe
☐ Safe Deposit Box No. __________
☐ Other Place ______________________________

☐ Kept by Accountant
Name ______________________________
Addr. ______________________________
____
Tele. ______________________________

All work sheets and/or evidence in support of tax returns are

☐ Attached to the tax return copies, which are located at the above.

☐ Located at:
____
____

Gift Tax Returns were filed for the following years:

________	________	________
________	________	________
________	________	________

All Gift Tax Returns with worksheets, appraisals, and other supporting evidence are located at: ______________________________
____

My Tax Acct/Lawyer is: ______________________________
____

Returns Audited by IRS for these years –		*Disposition of Audit*
	19	
	19	
	19	
	19	

OTHER INFORMATION

____
____
____

Additional Data from Page _____

CREDIT CARD LOG

FAMILY RECORD OF CREDIT CARDS

Credit Card Company	*Account Number*	*Cardholder's Name*	*Expiration Date*
American Express			
Bank Americard			
Master Charge			
Diner's Club			
Carte Blanche			

ADDITIONAL CREDIT CARD INFORMATION

Additional Data from Page _____

AUTOMOBILE DATA

Owner ____

Purchased From ______________________ Address ______________________

Date: ______________________ ______________________

Cost: ____________ Trade-in Allowance: ____________ Net Cost ____________

Make ____________ Model ____________ Color ____________

Serial # ______________________ Motor # ______________________

____

____

SERVICE DATA

Date	*Mileage*	*Service Center*	*Description of Services*

Additional Data from Page _____

AUTOMOBILE DATA

Owner ____

Purchased From ____________________ Address ____________________

Date: ____________________ ____________________

Cost: ____________ Trade-in Allowance: ____________ Net Cost ____________

Make ____________ Model ____________ Color ____________

Serial # ____________________ Motor # ____________________

____

____

SERVICE DATA

Date	*Mileage*	*Service Center*	*Description of Services*

Additional Data from Page _____

AUTOMOBILE DATA

Owner ____________________

Purchased From ____________________ Address ____________________

Date: ____________________ ____________________

Cost: __________ Trade-in Allowance: __________ Net Cost __________

Make __________ Model __________ Color __________

Serial # ____________________ Motor # ____________________

____

____

SERVICE DATA

Date	*Mileage*	*Service Center*	*Description of Services*

Additional Data from Page ____

AUTOMOBILE DATA

Owner ____

Purchased From ____________________ Address ____________________

Date: ____________________ ____________________

Cost: __________ Trade-in Allowance: __________ Net Cost __________

Make __________ Model __________ Color __________

Serial # ____________________ Motor # ____________________

____

____

SERVICE DATA

Date	*Mileage*	*Service Center*	*Description of Services*

Additional Data from Page _____

LAST WILL AND TESTAMENT INFORMATION

I (HAVE/HAVE NOT) made a WILL.

The ORIGINAL executed copy of my WILL, dated ___/___/___, is located at:

Addr. ______________________

______________________ Bank ______________________

______________________ Box # ______________________

The LAWYER who drew my WILL is: OR ☐ I wrote it MYSELF.

Name ______________________

Addr. ______________________

______________________ Tele. (____) ________

The WITNESSES to my WILL were:

Name ______________________ Tele. (____) ________

Name ______________________ Tele. (____) ________

Name ______________________ Tele. (____) ________

There is a CODICIL or ADDENDUM to my WILL ☐ YES ☐ NO, which is dated ___/___/___.

EXECUTOR(s)/EXECUTRIX of my WILL: ☐ Spouse and/or:

Name ______________________ Name ______________________

Addr. ______________________ Addr. ______________________

______________________ ______________________

DUPLICATE copy of my WILL is with above LAWYER or

Name ______________________ Name ______________________

Addr. ______________________ Addr. ______________________

______________________ ______________________

If COUNSEL is required for my ESTATE, I recommend:

Name ______________________ Name ______________________

Addr. ______________________ Addr. ______________________

______________________ ______________________

Additional Data from Page _____

LAST WILL AND TESTAMENT INFORMATION

I (HAVE/HAVE NOT) made a WILL.

The ORIGINAL executed copy of my WILL, dated ___/___/___, is located at:

Addr. ______________________________

______________________________ Bank ______________________________

______________________________ Box # ______________________________

The LAWYER who drew my WILL is: OR ☐ I wrote it MYSELF.

Name ______________________________

Addr. ______________________________

______________________________ Tele. (   ) __________

The WITNESSES to my WILL were:

Name ______________________________ Tele. (   ) __________

Name ______________________________ Tele. (   ) __________

Name ______________________________ Tele. (   ) __________

There is a CODICIL or ADDENDUM to my WILL ☐ YES ☐ NO, which is dated ___/___/___.

EXECUTOR(s)/EXECUTRIX of my WILL: ☐ Spouse and/or:

Name ______________________________ Name ______________________________

Addr. ______________________________ Addr. ______________________________

______________________________ ______________________________

DUPLICATE copy of my WILL is with above LAWYER or

Name ______________________________ Name ______________________________

Addr. ______________________________ Addr. ______________________________

______________________________ ______________________________

If COUNSEL is required for my ESTATE, I recommend:

Name ______________________________ Name ______________________________

Addr. ______________________________ Addr. ______________________________

______________________________ ______________________________

Additional Data from Page _____

LAST WILL AND TESTAMENT INFORMATION

I (HAVE/HAVE NOT) made a WILL.

The ORIGINAL executed copy of my WILL, dated ___/___/___, is located at:

Addr. ______________________

______________________ Bank ______________________

______________________ Box # ______________________

The LAWYER who drew my WILL is: OR ☐ I wrote it MYSELF.

Name ______________________

Addr. ______________________

______________________ Tele. (   ) ________

The WITNESSES to my WILL were:

Name ______________________ Tele. (   ) ________

Name ______________________ Tele. (   ) ________

Name ______________________ Tele. (   ) ________

There is a CODICIL or ADDENDUM to my WILL ☐ YES ☐ NO, which is dated ___/___/___.

EXECUTOR(s)/EXECUTRIX of my WILL: ☐ Spouse and/or:

Name ______________________ Name ______________________

Addr. ______________________ Addr. ______________________

______________________ ______________________

DUPLICATE copy of my WILL is with above LAWYER or

Name ______________________ Name ______________________

Addr. ______________________ Addr. ______________________

______________________ ______________________

If COUNSEL is required for my ESTATE, I recommend:

Name ______________________ Name ______________________

Addr. ______________________ Addr. ______________________

______________________ ______________________

Additional Data from Page _____

CHECKLIST – STEPS TO TAKE AFTER A FAMILY LOSS

- ☐ Delegate as Many Tasks as Possible to Relatives and Friends:
  - –Notifying Other Relatives, Fellow Employees, Out of Towners
  - –Answering Telephone and Keeping Record of Callers
  - –Looking after Young Children and Preparing Meals
- ☐ Discuss Arrangements with Funeral Director
- ☐ Obtain Several Copies of Death Certificate
- ☐ Arrange to See Lawyer and Executor and Start Probate of Will
- ☐ Review Death Benefit Claims and File for Same:
  - –Social Security
  - –Life Insurance
  - –Veterans Benefits
  - –Labor Union Benefits
  - –Fraternal or Social or Professional Organization Benefits
  - –Employer Benefits
- ☐ Contact Family Banker–Broker–Accountant
- ☐ Obtain Claim Forms from Life Insurance Companies
- ☐ Notify Insurer Carrying Deceased's Homeowners and Auto Insurance Policies
- ☐ Notify Personnel Department Where Deceased Was Employed
- ☐ Destroy Credit Cards
- ☐ Suspend any Open Orders with Stock Broker
- ☐ Search for Assets and Liabilities and Determine Location of Data
  - –Policies–Passbooks–Real Estate Deeds–Check Books
  - –Tax Returns–Auto Registrations–Loans and Payment Books
  - –Safe Deposit Boxes–Credit Insurance–Mortgage Insurance

Additional Data from Page _____

CHECKLIST—STEPS TO TAKE AFTER A FAMILY LOSS

- ☐ Open Estate Checking Account
- ☐ Pay Bills Owing by Decedent
- ☐ Obtain Trusted Counsel and Advice for Safekeeping and Investment of Assets
- ☐ Arrange for Proper Distribution of Assets to Rightful Heirs
- ☐ Carefully Consider Before Making any Gifts at This Time
- ☐ File Appropriate Tax and Estate Returns
- ☐ Send Note of Appreciation to All Who Attended and Assisted
- ☐ Pursue Normal Interests and Seek New Interests

Additional Data from Page _____

YOUR SOCIAL SECURITY ACCUMULATION

To find out how much you have in your Social Security account, send the following letter—there is *no charge* for this information:

Social Security Administration
P.O. Box 57
Baltimore, Maryland 21203

Gentlemen:

Please send me a statement of the amount of earnings recorded in my Social Security account.

Name ______________________________

Social Security No. ____–____–____

Date of Birth ____/____/____

Address ______________________________

City, State & Zip ______________________________

Signature ______________________________

WARNING!! Many people do not realize that there is a Statutory Limit of 3 years, 3 months, 15 days to correct any errors that may have been made in recording your earnings. Therefore, it is wise to request earnings information every 2½ to 3 years.

Additional Data from Page _____

PENSION AND RETIREMENT DATA

For ____________________

PENSION OR RETIREMENT PLAN IS COVERED THROUGH

____

____

Person to Contact ____________________

RETIREMENT BENEFITS UNDER THIS PLAN

____

____

____

____

____

____

____

Earliest Age Can Retire ____________________

LIFE INSURANCE AND OTHER BENEFITS IN PLAN

____

____

____

____

____

Name of Beneficiary Other Than Self ____________________

OPTIONAL METHODS AVAILABLE

____

____

____

OTHER INFORMATION

____

____

____

Additional Data from Page ____

PENSION AND RETIREMENT DATA

For ____

PENSION OR RETIREMENT PLAN IS COVERED THROUGH

____

____

Person to Contact ____

RETIREMENT BENEFITS UNDER THIS PLAN

____

____

____

____

____

____

____

Earliest Age Can Retire ____

LIFE INSURANCE AND OTHER BENEFITS IN PLAN

____

____

____

____

____

Name of Beneficiary Other Than Self ____

OPTIONAL METHODS AVAILABLE

____

____

____

OTHER INFORMATION

____

____

____

Additional Data from Page _____

PENSION AND RETIREMENT DATA

For ____

PENSION OR RETIREMENT PLAN IS COVERED THROUGH

____

____

Person to Contact ____

RETIREMENT BENEFITS UNDER THIS PLAN

____

____

____

____

____

____

____

Earliest Age Can Retire ____

LIFE INSURANCE AND OTHER BENEFITS IN PLAN

____

____

____

____

____

Name of Beneficiary Other Than Self ____

OPTIONAL METHODS AVAILABLE

____

____

____

OTHER INFORMATION

____

____

____

Additional Data from Page _____

IMPORTANT DATES TO REMEMBER

Use the pages in this section to annotate important dates to remember, such as, ANNIVERSARIES, BIRTHDAYS, DUE DATES, FINANCIAL INCOME DATES, SPECIAL OCCASIONS, SOCIAL, etc.

Month of JANUARY

Date	*Remember Because*

Month of FEBRUARY

Date	*Remember Because*

Additional Data from Page _____

IMPORTANT DATES TO REMEMBER

Use the pages in this section to annotate important dates to remember, such as, ANNIVERSARIES, BIRTHDAYS, DUE DATES, FINANCIAL INCOME DATES, SPECIAL OCCASIONS, SOCIAL, etc.

Month of MARCH		Month of APRIL	
Date	*Remember Because*	*Date*	*Remember Because*

Additional Data from Page _____

IMPORTANT DATES TO REMEMBER

Use the pages in this section to annotate important dates to remember, such as, ANNIVERSARIES, BIRTHDAYS, DUE DATES, FINANCIAL INCOME DATES, SPECIAL OCCASIONS, SOCIAL, etc.

Month of MAY

Date	*Remember Because*

Month of JUNE

Date	*Remember Because*

Additional Data from Page _____

IMPORTANT DATES TO REMEMBER

Use the pages in this section to annotate important dates to remember, such as, ANNIVERSARIES, BIRTHDAYS, DUE DATES, FINANCIAL INCOME DATES, SPECIAL OCCASIONS, SOCIAL, etc.

Month of JULY

Date	*Remember Because*

Month of AUGUST

Date	*Remember Because*

Additional Data from Page _____

IMPORTANT DATES TO REMEMBER

Use the pages in this section to annotate important dates to remember, such as, ANNIVERSARIES, BIRTHDAYS, DUE DATES, FINANCIAL INCOME DATES, SPECIAL OCCASIONS, SOCIAL, etc.

Month of SEPTEMBER

Date	*Remember Because*

Month of OCTOBER

Date	*Remember Because*

Additional Data from Page ____

IMPORTANT DATES TO REMEMBER

Use the pages in this section to annotate important dates to remember, such as, ANNIVERSARIES, BIRTHDAYS, DUE DATES, FINANCIAL INCOME DATES, SPECIAL OCCASIONS, SOCIAL, etc.

Month of NOVEMBER

Date	*Remember Because*

Month of DECEMBER

Date	*Remember Because*

Additional Data from Page ______

LIFETIME FAMILY DIARY

EVENTS AND HIGHLIGHTS

DATE	EVENTS	PHOTOGRAPHS

LIFETIME FAMILY DIARY

EVENTS AND HIGHLIGHTS

DATE	EVENTS	PHOTOGRAPHS

LIFETIME FAMILY DIARY

EVENTS AND HIGHLIGHTS

DATE	EVENTS	PHOTOGRAPHS

LIFETIME FAMILY DIARY

EVENTS AND HIGHLIGHTS

DATE	EVENTS	PHOTOGRAPHS

LIFETIME FAMILY DIARY

EVENTS AND HIGHLIGHTS

DATE	EVENTS	PHOTOGRAPHS

LIFETIME FAMILY DIARY

EVENTS AND HIGHLIGHTS

DATE	EVENTS	PHOTOGRAPHS

LIFETIME FAMILY DIARY

EVENTS AND HIGHLIGHTS

DATE	EVENTS	PHOTOGRAPHS

LIFETIME FAMILY DIARY

EVENTS AND HIGHLIGHTS

DATE	EVENTS	PHOTOGRAPHS

LIFETIME FAMILY DIARY

EVENTS AND HIGHLIGHTS

DATE	EVENTS	PHOTOGRAPHS

LIFETIME FAMILY DIARY

EVENTS AND HIGHLIGHTS

DATE	EVENTS	PHOTOGRAPHS

LIFETIME FAMILY DIARY

EVENTS AND HIGHLIGHTS

DATE	EVENTS	PHOTOGRAPHS

LIFETIME FAMILY DIARY

EVENTS AND HIGHLIGHTS

DATE	EVENTS	PHOTOGRAPHS

LIFETIME FAMILY DIARY

EVENTS AND HIGHLIGHTS

DATE	EVENTS	PHOTOGRAPHS

LIFETIME FAMILY DIARY

EVENTS AND HIGHLIGHTS

DATE	EVENTS	PHOTOGRAPHS

LIFETIME FAMILY DIARY

EVENTS AND HIGHLIGHTS

DATE	EVENTS	PHOTOGRAPHS

LIFETIME FAMILY DIARY

EVENTS AND HIGHLIGHTS

DATE	EVENTS	PHOTOGRAPHS

LIFETIME FAMILY DIARY

EVENTS AND HIGHLIGHTS

DATE	EVENTS	PHOTOGRAPHS

LIFETIME FAMILY DIARY

EVENTS AND HIGHLIGHTS

DATE	EVENTS	PHOTOGRAPHS

LIFETIME FAMILY DIARY

EVENTS AND HIGHLIGHTS

DATE	EVENTS	PHOTOGRAPHS

LIFETIME FAMILY DIARY

EVENTS AND HIGHLIGHTS

DATE	EVENTS	PHOTOGRAPHS

LIFETIME FAMILY DIARY

EVENTS AND HIGHLIGHTS

DATE	EVENTS	PHOTOGRAPHS

LIFETIME FAMILY DIARY

EVENTS AND HIGHLIGHTS

DATE	EVENTS	PHOTOGRAPHS

LIFETIME FAMILY DIARY

EVENTS AND HIGHLIGHTS

DATE	EVENTS	PHOTOGRAPHS

LIFETIME FAMILY DIARY

EVENTS AND HIGHLIGHTS

DATE	EVENTS	PHOTOGRAPHS

LIFETIME FAMILY DIARY

EVENTS AND HIGHLIGHTS

DATE	EVENTS	PHOTOGRAPHS

LIFETIME FAMILY DIARY

EVENTS AND HIGHLIGHTS

DATE	EVENTS	PHOTOGRAPHS

LIFETIME FAMILY DIARY

EVENTS AND HIGHLIGHTS

DATE	EVENTS	PHOTOGRAPHS

LIFETIME FAMILY DIARY

EVENTS AND HIGHLIGHTS

DATE	EVENTS	PHOTOGRAPHS

LIFETIME FAMILY DIARY

EVENTS AND HIGHLIGHTS

DATE	EVENTS	PHOTOGRAPHS

LIFETIME FAMILY DIARY

EVENTS AND HIGHLIGHTS

DATE	EVENTS	PHOTOGRAPHS

FAMILY RECIPES

Obtained From: ITEM:

Ingredients and Quantities Instructions

Obtained From: ITEM:

Ingredients and Quantities Instructions

Obtained From: ITEM:

Ingredients and Quantities Instructions

FAMILY RECIPES

Obtained From:

ITEM:

Ingredients and Quantities

Instructions

Obtained From:

ITEM:

Ingredients and Quantities

Instructions

Obtained From:

ITEM:

Ingredients and Quantities

Instructions

FAMILY RECIPES

Obtained From: ITEM:

Ingredients and Quantities Instructions

Obtained From: ITEM:

Ingredients and Quantities Instructions

Obtained From: ITEM:

Ingredients and Quantities Instructions

FAMILY RECIPES

Obtained From: ITEM:

Ingredients and Quantities Instructions

Obtained From: ITEM:

Ingredients and Quantities Instructions

Obtained From: ITEM:

Ingredients and Quantities Instructions

FAMILY RECIPES

Obtained From:

ITEM:

Ingredients and Quantities

Instructions

Obtained From:

ITEM:

Ingredients and Quantities

Instructions

Obtained From:

ITEM:

Ingredients and Quantities

Instructions

FAMILY RECIPES

Obtained From: ITEM:

Ingredients and Quantities Instructions

Obtained From: ITEM:

Ingredients and Quantities Instructions

Obtained From: ITEM:

Ingredients and Quantities Instructions

TRAVEL/VACATION LOG

DESTINATION

Date Departed: ____________________

Date Returned: ____________________

Family/Friends in Your Group:

1. ____________________
2. ____________________
3. ____________________
4. ____________________
5. ____________________
6. ____________________
7. ____________________
8. ____________________

HIGHLIGHTS

DESTINATION

Date Departed: ____________________

Date Returned: ____________________

Family/Friends in Your Group:

1. ____________________
2. ____________________
3. ____________________
4. ____________________
5. ____________________
6. ____________________
7. ____________________
8. ____________________

HIGHLIGHTS

TRAVEL/VACATION LOG

DESTINATION

Date Departed:____________________
Date Returned:____________________
Family/Friends in Your Group:

1.____________________
2.____________________
3.____________________
4.____________________
5.____________________
6.____________________
7.____________________
8.____________________

HIGHLIGHTS

DESTINATION

Date Departed:____________________
Date Returned:____________________
Family/Friends in Your Group:

1.____________________
2.____________________
3.____________________
4.____________________
5.____________________
6.____________________
7.____________________
8.____________________

HIGHLIGHTS

TRAVEL/VACATION LOG

DESTINATION

Date Departed: ____________________

Date Returned: ____________________

Family/Friends in Your Group:

1. ____________________
2. ____________________
3. ____________________
4. ____________________
5. ____________________
6. ____________________
7. ____________________
8. ____________________

HIGHLIGHTS

____
____
____
____
____
____
____
____
____
____
____
____
____

DESTINATION

Date Departed: ____________________

Date Returned: ____________________

Family/Friends in Your Group:

1. ____________________
2. ____________________
3. ____________________
4. ____________________
5. ____________________
6. ____________________
7. ____________________
8. ____________________

HIGHLIGHTS

____
____
____
____
____
____
____
____
____
____
____
____
____

TRAVEL/VACATION LOG

DESTINATION

Date Departed:________________

Date Returned:________________

Family/Friends in Your Group:

1.________________
2.________________
3.________________
4.________________
5.________________
6.________________
7.________________
8.________________

HIGHLIGHTS

DESTINATION

Date Departed:________________

Date Returned:________________

Family/Friends in Your Group:

1.________________
2.________________
3.________________
4.________________
5.________________
6.________________
7.________________
8.________________

HIGHLIGHTS

TRAVEL/VACATION LOG

DESTINATION

Date Departed: ____________________

Date Returned: ____________________

Family/Friends in Your Group:

1. ____________________
2. ____________________
3. ____________________
4. ____________________
5. ____________________
6. ____________________
7. ____________________
8. ____________________

HIGHLIGHTS

DESTINATION

Date Departed: ____________________

Date Returned: ____________________

Family/Friends in Your Group:

1. ____________________
2. ____________________
3. ____________________
4. ____________________
5. ____________________
6. ____________________
7. ____________________
8. ____________________

HIGHLIGHTS

TRAVEL/VACATION LOG

DESTINATION

Date Departed:____________________

Date Returned:____________________

Family/Friends in Your Group:

1. ____________________
2. ____________________
3. ____________________
4. ____________________
5. ____________________
6. ____________________
7. ____________________
8. ____________________

HIGHLIGHTS

DESTINATION

Date Departed:____________________

Date Returned:____________________

Family/Friends in Your Group:

1. ____________________
2. ____________________
3. ____________________
4. ____________________
5. ____________________
6. ____________________
7. ____________________
8. ____________________

HIGHLIGHTS

TRAVEL/VACATION LOG

DESTINATION

Date Departed:____________________

Date Returned:____________________

Family/Friends in Your Group:

1. ____________________
2. ____________________
3. ____________________
4. ____________________
5. ____________________
6. ____________________
7. ____________________
8. ____________________

HIGHLIGHTS

DESTINATION

Date Departed:____________________

Date Returned:____________________

Family/Friends in Your Group:

1. ____________________
2. ____________________
3. ____________________
4. ____________________
5. ____________________
6. ____________________
7. ____________________
8. ____________________

HIGHLIGHTS

TRAVEL/VACATION LOG

DESTINATION

Date Departed:____________________

Date Returned:____________________

Family/Friends in Your Group:

1.
2.
3.
4.
5.
6.
7.
8.

HIGHLIGHTS

DESTINATION

Date Departed:____________________

Date Returned:____________________

Family/Friends in Your Group:

1.
2.
3.
4.
5.
6.
7.
8.

HIGHLIGHTS

TRAVEL/VACATION LOG

DESTINATION

Date Departed:____________________

Date Returned:____________________

Family/Friends in Your Group:

1. ____________________
2. ____________________
3. ____________________
4. ____________________
5. ____________________
6. ____________________
7. ____________________
8. ____________________

HIGHLIGHTS

DESTINATION

Date Departed:____________________

Date Returned:____________________

Family/Friends in Your Group:

1. ____________________
2. ____________________
3. ____________________
4. ____________________
5. ____________________
6. ____________________
7. ____________________
8. ____________________

HIGHLIGHTS

TRAVEL/VACATION LOG

DESTINATION

Date Departed:________________
Date Returned:________________
Family/Friends in Your Group:

1. ________________
2. ________________
3. ________________
4. ________________
5. ________________
6. ________________
7. ________________
8. ________________

HIGHLIGHTS

DESTINATION

Date Departed:________________
Date Returned:________________
Family/Friends in Your Group:

1. ________________
2. ________________
3. ________________
4. ________________
5. ________________
6. ________________
7. ________________
8. ________________

HIGHLIGHTS

TRAVEL/VACATION LOG

DESTINATION

Date Departed:____________________
Date Returned:____________________
Family/Friends in Your Group:

1. ____________________
2. ____________________
3. ____________________
4. ____________________
5. ____________________
6. ____________________
7. ____________________
8. ____________________

HIGHLIGHTS

DESTINATION

Date Departed:____________________
Date Returned:____________________
Family/Friends in Your Group:

1. ____________________
2. ____________________
3. ____________________
4. ____________________
5. ____________________
6. ____________________
7. ____________________
8. ____________________

HIGHLIGHTS

PET HISTORY

Name:

Place:

Date of Birth:

Breed:

Other Data:

Markings:

How Obtained:

MEDICAL HISTORY

SHOTS RECEIVED

DATE	DESCRIPTION	LOCATION

AILMENTS

Date	Description	Treatment

VISITS TO VETERINARIAN

DATE	VET	Period of Stay	SERVICES RECEIVED	COST	COMMENTS

PET HISTORY

Name: ______________________ Place: ______________________

Date of Birth: ______________________

Breed: ______________________ Other Data: ______________________

Markings: ______________________

How Obtained: ______________________

MEDICAL HISTORY

SHOTS RECEIVED

DATE	DESCRIPTION	LOCATION

AILMENTS

Date	Description	Treatment

VISITS TO VETERINARIAN

DATE	VET	Period of Stay	SERVICES RECEIVED	COST	COMMENTS

PET HISTORY

Name:
Place:
Date of Birth:
Breed:
Other Data:
Markings:
How Obtained:

MEDICAL HISTORY

SHOTS RECEIVED

DATE	DESCRIPTION	LOCATION

AILMENTS

Date	Description	Treatment

VISITS TO VETERINARIAN

DATE	VET	Period of Stay	SERVICES RECEIVED	COST	COMMENTS

PET HISTORY

Name: ______________________ Place: ______________________

Date of Birth: ______________________

Breed: ______________________ Other Data: ______________________

Markings: ______________________

How Obtained: ______________________

MEDICAL HISTORY		
SHOTS RECEIVED		
DATE	DESCRIPTION	LOCATION

AILMENTS		
Date	Description	Treatment

VISITS TO VETERINARIAN

DATE	VET	Period of Stay	SERVICES RECEIVED	COST	COMMENTS

PET HISTORY

Name: ____________________ Place: ____________________

Date of Birth: ____________________

Breed: ____________________ Other Data: ____________________

Markings: ____________________

How Obtained: ____________________

MEDICAL HISTORY

SHOTS RECEIVED

DATE	DESCRIPTION	LOCATION

AILMENTS

Date	Description	Treatment

VISITS TO VETERINARIAN

DATE	VET	Period of Stay	SERVICES RECEIVED	COST	COMMENTS

PET HISTORY

Name: ____________________ Place: ____________________

Date of Birth: ____________________

Breed: ____________________ Other Data: ____________________

Markings: ____________________

How Obtained: ____________________

MEDICAL HISTORY

SHOTS RECEIVED

DATE	DESCRIPTION	LOCATION

AILMENTS

Date	Description	Treatment

VISITS TO VETERINARIAN

DATE	VET	Period of Stay	SERVICES RECEIVED	COST	COMMENTS

PET HISTORY

Name:

Place:

Date of Birth:

Breed:

Other Data:

Markings:

How Obtained:

MEDICAL HISTORY

SHOTS RECEIVED

DATE	DESCRIPTION	LOCATION

AILMENTS

Date	Description	Treatment

VISITS TO VETERINARIAN

DATE	VET	Period of Stay	SERVICES RECEIVED	COST	COMMENTS

PET HISTORY

Name: ______________________ Place: ______________________

Date of Birth: ______________________

Breed: ______________________ Other Data: ______________________

Markings: ______________________

How Obtained: ______________________

MEDICAL HISTORY			AILMENTS		
SHOTS RECEIVED			Date	Description	Treatment
DATE	DESCRIPTION	LOCATION			

VISITS TO VETERINARIAN

DATE	VET	Period of Stay	SERVICES RECEIVED	COST	COMMENTS

PET HISTORY

Name: ______________________ Place: ______________________

Date of Birth: ______________________

Breed: ______________________ Other Data: ______________________

Markings: ______________________

How Obtained: ______________________

MEDICAL HISTORY

SHOTS RECEIVED

DATE	DESCRIPTION	LOCATION

AILMENTS

Date	Description	Treatment

VISITS TO VETERINARIAN

DATE	VET	Period of Stay	SERVICES RECEIVED	COST	COMMENTS

PET HISTORY

Name: ______ Place: ______

Date of Birth: ______

Breed: ______ Other Data: ______

Markings: ______

How Obtained: ______

MEDICAL HISTORY

SHOTS RECEIVED

DATE	DESCRIPTION	LOCATION

AILMENTS

Date	Description	Treatment

VISITS TO VETERINARIAN

DATE	VET	Period of Stay	SERVICES RECEIVED	COST	COMMENTS

ADDENDUM

ADDENDUM

ADDENDUM

ADDENDUM

ADDENDUM

ADDENDUM

ADDENDUM

ADDENDUM

ADDENDUM